WATERWAY WEST

WATERWAY WEST

The Story of the Erie Canal

Mary Kay Phelan

ILLUSTRATED BY

David Frampton

THOMAS Y. CROWELL COMPANY

NEW YORK

copy (1)

For my husband, Marty,
whose enthusiasm
for the Erie has meant so much

 Published simultaneously in Canada by Fitzhenry & Whiteside Limited, Toronto.
Manufactured in the United States of America

Library of Congress Cataloging in Publication Data
Phelan, Mary Kay. Waterway west.
Bibliography: p. Includes index.
1. Erie Canal—History—Juvenile literature.
I. Frampton, David. II. Title.
HE396.E6P47 386'.48'09747 77-1787
ISBN 0-690-01333-7
1 2 3 4 5 6 7 8 9 10

Acknowledgments

In recounting the story of the Erie Canal—the politics involved, as well as the progress of construction—letters, diaries, and newspapers of the day have been most helpful. All conversations are based on reports of the participants. Nothing has been fictionized.

Of primary importance in my research were three volumes: *Memoir of DeWitt Clinton* by David Hosack, with its lengthy appendix containing original documents concerning Clinton's life; *Laws of The State of New York in Relation to the Erie Canal with Annual Reports of Canal Commissioners;* and the *Memoir* by Cadwallader Colden, published in 1825, in which the author gives a detailed day-by-day account of the Wedding of the Waters.

Other Books by
Mary Kay Phelan

The Burning of Washington: August 1814
Four Days in Philadelphia—1776
Midnight Alarm: The Story of Paul Revere's Ride
Mr. Lincoln's Inaugural Journey
The Story of the Boston Massacre
The Story of the Boston Tea Party
The Story of the Great Chicago Fire, 1871

Contents

WATERWAY WEST

CHAPTER I

Initial Stirrings

1809

A worried frown creases the brow of Judge Joshua Forman as the stagecoach jounces along the last few miles leading into Washington City. The past six days have been trying ones for the judge. His mission is such an important one—but will he be able to accomplish it?

It was less than two weeks ago—in January, 1809—that the New York state legislature had appointed Judge Forman to call on President Thomas Jefferson and to seek support and funds from the national government to build a canal across upstate New York. The judge then immediately wrote Congressman William Kirkpatrick, his old friend from Salina in upstate New York. Would he please arrange an appointment with Mr. Jefferson? A few days later, Forman left the state capital at Albany, confident he could interest the President in the project.

It's been a long and tedious trip—sailing down the Hudson River to New York City, taking the stagecoach line that leads through Philadelphia and on toward the nine-year-old federal capital. The judge has been riding twelve hours a day over rutted roads, stopping late at night in wayside taverns and getting up before dawn to continue his journey. Now Forman is beginning to wonder whether all this travel will have been for nothing. He shrugs off his pessimistic mood. It's probably because he's so weary. After a good night's rest, he'll call at the President's House tomorrow and present his most persuasive arguments.

There are good arguments for the necessity of a Canal. The way west has long been a difficult one for the people of this young nation. The rugged chain of Appalachian Mountains forms a barrier that stretches from Canada into the Deep South, thus dividing the country. It *is* possible to cross these mountains; there are many daring pioneers who have done so. But the trip requires courage, stamina, and money for equipment. Then, too, there's always the danger of Indian raids.

Practically the only northern break in this barrier is located in New York State—in the valley where the Hudson and Mohawk rivers meet. Those who try this route by boat find that travel up the Hudson poses no problem. The river is wide and calm. But at the point where the two waterways meet, just north of Albany, the Mohawk is filled with swirling rapids and massive rocks. People going west must hire a wagon to transfer themselves and their possessions over a rough trail into Schenectady, seventeen miles distant, where the river again becomes passable.

This procedure of switching from boat to wagon and back again must be repeated several times before the traveler reaches Buffalo and can gain passage to the west by way of Lake Erie. To add to the hazards, most of the route is surrounded by dense forests. The sparse settlements have only a scattering of cabins. And west of Rome there are treacherous swamplands where sickness becomes rampant during the summer months. Despite all the difficulties, this has become the easiest way to cross the state of New York.

One of the first suggestions for a canal that would join Lake Erie with the Hudson River came from Gouverneur Morris, a member of the First Continental Congress. In the summer of 1777 he visited the Revolutionary Army encampment at Fort Edward, north of Troy. Later, recounting a conversation he had with the officers there, Morris described how the Mohawk River joins the Hudson from the west. In poetic language he envisioned that "once freed from a foreign yoke" there would come a day "when the waters of the great western inland seas would, by the aid of man, break through their barriers and mingle with those of the Hudson."

Casual discussion of inland waterways continued, although it was nine years before the New York state legislature passed a bill "for establishing and opening lock navigation within this state." Two companies were incorporated and financed by private capital. Both failed, but not before some progress was made in providing better transportation along the Mohawk River.

Gouverneur Morris was still agitating for a canal that would link Lake Erie with the Hudson. In the summer of 1800 he journeyed across the state, following the Mohawk. Upon reaching Fort Erie, near Buffalo, he stood on the lake shore and counted nine vessels riding at anchor. The sight made such an impression that after returning home he wrote his friend, John Parish, in Hamburg, Germany:

Does it not seem like magic? Yet this magic is but the early effort of victorious industry. Hundreds of large ships will in no distant period bound on the billows of those inland seas. . . . As yet, my friend, we only crawl along the outer shell of our country. The interior excels the part we inhabit in soil, in climate, in everything. The proudest empire in Europe is but a bauble compared to what American will *be,* must *be in the course of two centuries, perhaps of one.*

It was only two years ago, in 1807, that the idea of a canal linking Lake Erie with the Hudson River was first mentioned by a newspaper. The *Genesee Messenger* of Canandaigua, New York, published a series of fourteen essays written by Jesse Hawley. The author had been a flour merchant in Geneva, New York, until the high cost of shipping bankrupted his business. He then fled to Pittsburgh to escape his creditors but later returned to give himself up. As a result, he was confined in the county jail at Canandaigua for twenty months.

To combat his despondency, Hawley "resolved to publish to the world my favorite, fanciful project of an overland canal, for the benefit of my country. . . ." Only a few books and maps were available to him, but after careful study he plotted a route across the state, estimating the cost of construction to be about six million dollars. Using the pen name "Hercules," he predicted that tremendous advantages would come to the state of New York. Land would be developed; property values would rise; and population would increase along the canal route. "No situation on the globe," he concluded, "offers such extensive and numerous advantages to inland navigation by a canal as this. . . . Nor do I conceive the idea to be vain, or even incorrect in saying that it appears as if the Author of nature . . . had in prospect a large and valuable canal . . . to be completed at some period in the history of man, by his ingenuity and industry."

With the publication of Hawley's essays, the canal proposal began to receive more serious attention from the public. There was much talk about expansion. Certainly an inland waterway would contribute to trade possibilities. During the 1808 session of the state legislature, Judge Forman introduced a resolution favoring the building of a canal across upstate New York.

Some members of the New York Assembly (the lower house) reacted "with such expressions of surprise and ridicule as are due to a very wild and foolish subject." The proposed canal was nearly twenty times as long as any yet completed in this country. Who would dare attempt such a feat through the vast wilderness of forests and swamps? How could such a project be accomplished with only hand shovels and plows? Those members opposed to the venture brushed it off as too stupendous for serious consideration.

Nevertheless, there were some farsighted legislators who believed the recommendation was worth looking into. "It could do no harm, and might do some good" was the consensus among the pro-canal members.

After several days of heated debate, a tentative survey of proposed canal routes was authorized by both houses. Six hundred dollars was appropriated for expenses, and Judge James Geddes was appointed to make the survey.

Geddes, a native of Onondaga County, is a former state legislator who has practiced law and dabbled in surveying as a hobby. Pleased with the assignment, he began his travels almost at once, measuring the horizontal and vertical angles of hills and valleys between the Hudson River and Lake Erie. After meticulous exploration of various routes, Geddes returned early in December 1808 to write a scholarly report for the surveyor general. He was convinced, he stated, of "the complete feasibility and utter desirability of leading an artificial waterway over the more equable and therefore less expensive levels to the southward, directly to Lake Erie."

Judge Forman was pleased with Geddes' report. It was exactly what he hoped for. During the first weeks of this month of January 1809, Forman spent many hours with Geddes, discussing the surveyor's conclusions. The judge wanted to be well informed when he called on President Jefferson.

Now the journey from Albany is almost over. The stagecoach rumbles through the outskirts of Washington City and soon turns into Pennsylvania Avenue, the main thoroughfare that leads from the Capitol to the President's House. In the darkness Judge Forman is able to see only the outlines of the tall Lombardy poplars lining the street. He remembers that two years ago the President asked Congress for an appropriation to beautify the avenue. Certainly the trees must be a vast improvement.

When his conveyance lurches to a stop at one of the new inns on the avenue, the judge clambers out, trying to unkink his cramped legs. Entering the inn, he signs the registry and sends a messenger to William Kirkpatrick's boardinghouse, asking the congressman to come around tomorrow as early as possible.

It is nearly nine o'clock the next morning when Kirkpatrick knocks on the judge's door. After a hearty handshake, the legislator says that President Jefferson will see them at eleven. Meanwhile he'd like to take a look at Geddes' report.

Forman pulls out a sheaf of papers from his satchel and hands them to his friend. The further Kirkpatrick reads, the more enthusiastic he becomes. Yes, certainly the President should be impressed. Such a proposal has great possibilities, not only for the state of New York, but for the entire nation as well. Then glancing at his pocket watch, the legislator remarks that it's time to go if they are to keep their appointment.

As the two men leave the inn, Kirkpatrick gestures

toward the new Capitol at the east end of Pennsylvania Avenue. The two stately buildings are much more impressive than the judge had expected. The one to the north is for the Senate, his friend explains; it was the only building completed when the seat of government moved here in November 1800. But last year the south wing was finished and is now occupied by the House of Representatives. The two are connected by a wooden walkway, although the architect, William Thornton, has designed a handsome rotunda that will replace the walkway in the near future.

Despite the strong January winds, the men stride briskly west along Pennsylvania Avenue. It is not long before the President's House looms into sight. A stone wall encircles the grounds around the sandstone mansion. Turning in through the gateposts topped by bronze eagles, they approach the north entrance. Kirkpatrick points out the long low-lying wings, disguised behind classic colonnades, running east and west from the main building. These, he says, were designed by Mr. Jefferson and provide space for stables, a meathouse, an icehouse, and storage rooms for wines, coal, and wood. Everyone thinks they are a distinctive architectural addition.

In answer to their knock, the men are greeted by the official doorkeeper, Jean Pierre Soussiant. The handsome young refugee who fled his native land several years ago is now employed by Mr. Jefferson.

French John, as he is called, ushers them into the oval drawing room where the President is waiting, his pet mocking bird perched on his shoulder.

Congressman Kirkpatrick introduces Judge Forman, and the men shake hands. The judge remarks that the house is much larger than he had expected. "Yes," says the President with a chuckle. "I tell my friends it's big enough for two emperors, one Pope, and the Grand Lama." Only twenty-three rooms are furnished, he explains. The great audience room is still not completed. There is much to be done, but he'll be leaving office soon. Then President-elect Madison and his wife, Dolley, will have the pleasure of living here.

After this exchange of pleasantries, Judge Forman launches into the purpose of his call. He reminds the President that only last year Secretary of the Treasury Albert Gallatin had prepared a report on the subject of internal improvements. This had included the recommendation for a system of canals that would promote better communication between the Atlantic coast and the Great Lakes.

Further, the judge says, the state of New York has explored the route of a canal from the Hudson River to Lake Erie and finds it practical. Such a canal will not only assist in settlement of western lands but will also provide a channel for trade that will unite the country.

Because Secretary Gallatin in his report suggested a national expenditure of some two million dollars, Forman and Kirkpatrick hope that Mr. Jefferson will feel that the proposed canal is entitled to financial help from the national government. President Jefferson listens in silence as the men present their case.

When they finish, the President shakes his head. "It's a very fine project, and might be executed a century hence," he says. "But here is a canal of a few miles, projected by General Washington, which, if completed, would render this a fine commercial city, which has languished for many years because the small sum of two hundred thousand dollars necessary to complete it, cannot be obtained from the general government, the state government, or from individuals—and you talk of making a canal of three hundred and fifty miles through the wilderness. *It is little short of madness to think of it at this day*."

Such strong words leave no doubt about the President's refusal. Nevertheless, as the legislators leave, Judge Forman turns to Mr. Jefferson. "Having conceived the idea, ascertained its practicability, and in some measure appreciated its importance," he says, "I think the state of New York will never rest until it is accomplished."

CHAPTER 2

Exploration of an Idea

1810–1812

Judge Forman and Congressman Kirkpatrick leave the President's House, disappointed but not disheartened. They agree that Mr. Jefferson has been short-sighted in refusing to give his assistance to the project. It is evident that he is far more interested in a canal that would join the Potomac with the Ohio River and benefit his native state of Virginia.

When the judge returns to Albany, he is gratified to find that the proposal for an inland waterway has become a popular subject for discussion. Editors, civic leaders, even clergymen, are now expressing opinions—whether for or against it. There's much controversy, but at least the idea is no longer dismissed as a wild and ridiculous dream.

Debate among politicians continues throughout the

year, though nothing specific is accomplished. The project is not one sponsored by either the Federalists or the Antifederalists. Members of both factions find themselves crossing party lines on the issue. One evening in late February 1810, there is a particularly hectic session in the Senate. Afterward, Jonas Platt, leader of the Federalist faction, approaches his friend Senator Thomas Eddy. If such an ambitious project is ever to be approved, says Platt, it will only come about through bipartisan cooperation. A strong political figure from the opposite party is needed, an Antifederalist who is influential throughout the state. Why not enlist De Witt Clinton?

Eddy considers the suggestion thoughtfully. Yes, De Witt Clinton *is* well-known. At forty-one years of age, he's had a distinguished political career, first serving as a member of the state legislature and later as a United States senator from New York. Furthermore he's had several terms as mayor of New York City. Just a few months ago political opponents succeeded in ousting Clinton from that office, but he still holds a seat in the state senate.

De Witt Clinton is a skillful politician with a driving ambition, Platt points out. He's known for his persistence in getting projects accomplished. Though sometimes ruthless and overbearing in manner, Clinton is often quoted as saying, "The meekness of Quakerism will do in religion, but not in politics."

He's also a man of varied interests, a perpetual scholar whose studies range from natural history to science and the arts. Certainly a man with these qualifications would be an asset to the canal project.

Senator Eddy nods approval.

"And there must be a board of commissioners to examine and survey the routes," Platt continues. "Our object should be to balance the opposing political parties as nearly as possible, and to combine talents, influences, and wealth in constituting this board."

Further discussion follows as legislators agree on the men to designate as commissioners. Platt says he will prepare a resolution to present to the senate. But first they must request an interview with the one person who is essential to their project.

The following evening the two senators call on De Witt Clinton at the boardinghouse where he resides while in Albany. The man who answers their knock is a slim handsome figure. His erect stature makes him seem even taller than his six-foot three-inch height. Beneath a thatch of curly brown hair, the facial features are classic. There's a frankness about the wide-set dark eyes, a friendliness in the generously curving mouth.

The visitors waste no time in explaining the purpose of tonight's visit. Armed with reports and plans, Senator Platt sketches the background of the canal project—the difficulties faced by people wanting to move into the western lands, the lack of trade because of transportation difficulties. If an artificial waterway can be built, he says, it will benefit not only New York State but the entire nation. Such a project, though, will never receive legislative approval without bipartisan cooperation. Will Clinton agree to participate?

There is a long silence as De Witt Clinton considers carefully their proposition. Finally he answers, "I am in great measure a stranger to the western interior of our state. I have given but little attention to the subject of canal navigation, but the exposition of your plan strikes my mind with great force. I am prepared to say that it is an object worthy of thorough examination."

Platt then suggests that he will present to the legislature a resolution requesting that a bipartisan canal commission be established. The members, he adds, should be men of wealth and public spirit who will serve without compensation. Thus the only appropriation needed will be for the expenses of the engineers and surveyors employed by the commission. The purpose of such a commission will be to explore and survey the proposed routes and report their findings to the legislators. Without hesitation, Clinton promises to second the resolution.

During the next few weeks, De Witt Clinton seeks

out everything he can find on the subject of canals. He studies the history of European waterways and writes several foreign engineers for advice on construction. He procures surveyors' maps of New York State and scrutinizes the terrain in great detail. He pores over the fourteen lengthy essays written three years ago by Jesse Hawley. The more he reads, the more convinced he is that the canal must become a reality. Settlement of the west is imperative, if this nation is to become strong. And an artificial waterway through upper New York would surely bring both honor and prosperity to his native state.

During the senate session on March 12, Jonas Platt presents his resolution, and Clinton seconds it. Two days later it is adopted by both houses of the legislature, and the commission is appointed. The members are Gouverneur Morris, Stephen Van Rensselaer, Simeon De Witt, Will North, Thomas Eddy, Peter B. Porter, and De Witt Clinton.

From New York City on June 30, Thomas Eddy and De Witt Clinton set out for Albany where the members of the commission will meet to plan their survey of the various routes. They book passage on the *Paragon*, Robert Fulton's steamboat. (His first, the *Clermont*, made its initial voyage only three years ago.) At present the *Paragon* makes regularly scheduled trips up and down the Hudson River. For the two men this is a novel experience; it's also much faster—thirty hours traveling time compared to the several days required on a sailing vessel.

Promptly at nine o'clock on the morning of July 2, Eddy and Clinton join the other commission members in Simeon De Witt's office. The group is a distinguished one. Clinton's cousin, Simeon De Witt has already made a notable record as surveyor general for the state of New York. Stephen Van Rensselaer, owner of a vast estate in the Hudson Valley, is known for his political influence and his genuine interest in public works. General William North, a Revolutionary War veteran, has an enviable reputation as both a politician and a man of integrity. Thomas Eddy has had some experience in canal building; it's believed his knowledge will be of real assistance.

Because of notable public service both at home and abroad, Gouverneur Morris is elected to head the group. Only one member of the commission is absent; Peter B. Porter, representative from the western edge of the state, will await the other members' arrival at his home in Black Rock on the Niagara River, four and a half miles north of Buffalo. Also present this morning is Judge James Geddes, who made the initial survey two years ago. He has consented to be the commission's consultant and will accompany them on the trip west.

In the past years two major routes have been proposed—one to connect the Hudson directly with Lake Erie, the other to link the Hudson with Lake Ontario. In all fairness, the commissioners agree that both routes must be thoroughly explored.

Soon after sunrise on July 3, the members set out on the first leg of their hazardous surveying journey—from Albany to Rome. During the thirteen-mile trip to Schenectady they begin to realize the terrible traveling conditions for those going west—riding in a lurching stagecoach that carries them along bumpy paths through dark stretches of forest.

At Schenectady, where the Mohawk River becomes passable, the commissioners transfer to river boats. Now the trip becomes even more tedious. Often the wind dies down, and the small vessels must be propelled by attendants with poles. Food is a problem. Each man has brought both a fishing rod and a gun, so most of what they eat is either caught in the river or shot in the forest. Since there are no sleeping facilities on board, the boats pull inland at night, and the members pitch tents for a few hours of rest.

During these stops they often talk with the local inhabitants about what improvements a canal could make in their lives. They will no longer be isolated. Towns will spring up; population will increase. Being able to transport their produce on the canal will bring riches beyond their wildest dreams.

Most people are skeptical, brushing it off as wild

talk. Still, they are curious. For instance, asks one farmer, how is it possible for boats to drop from the height of Lake Erie to the level of the Hudson River? Why, it's hundreds of feet! No boat could take a nose dive like that and have the passengers survive.

Indeed, no, agrees De Witt Clinton. The boats will be floated up or down by a series of locks, much like those that have been built in Europe. A lock, he explains, is like an obling stone box built into a canal. There are watertight gates at either end of it.

When a boat approaches from a higher level, the gate is opened, and the vessel moves into the box; the gate is then closed behind it. There are huge pipes buried under the lock. Slowly, very slowly, the water is drained through these outlet pipes until it reaches the same low level as the water on the opposite end of the lock. Then the gate is opened, and the boat moves out at the lower level to continue the trip on the waterway.

To illustrate his explanation, Clinton draws a sketch of a canalboat being lowered by means of a lock. If the boat must climb up, he adds, the process is merely reversed. There are times, too, when the ascent or decent is too steep for one lock. In that case there will have to be several locks resembling a giant stairway.

Though the listeners are polite, most remain skeptical. There's too much wilderness land, they mutter. To clear out the dense forests and build an artificial

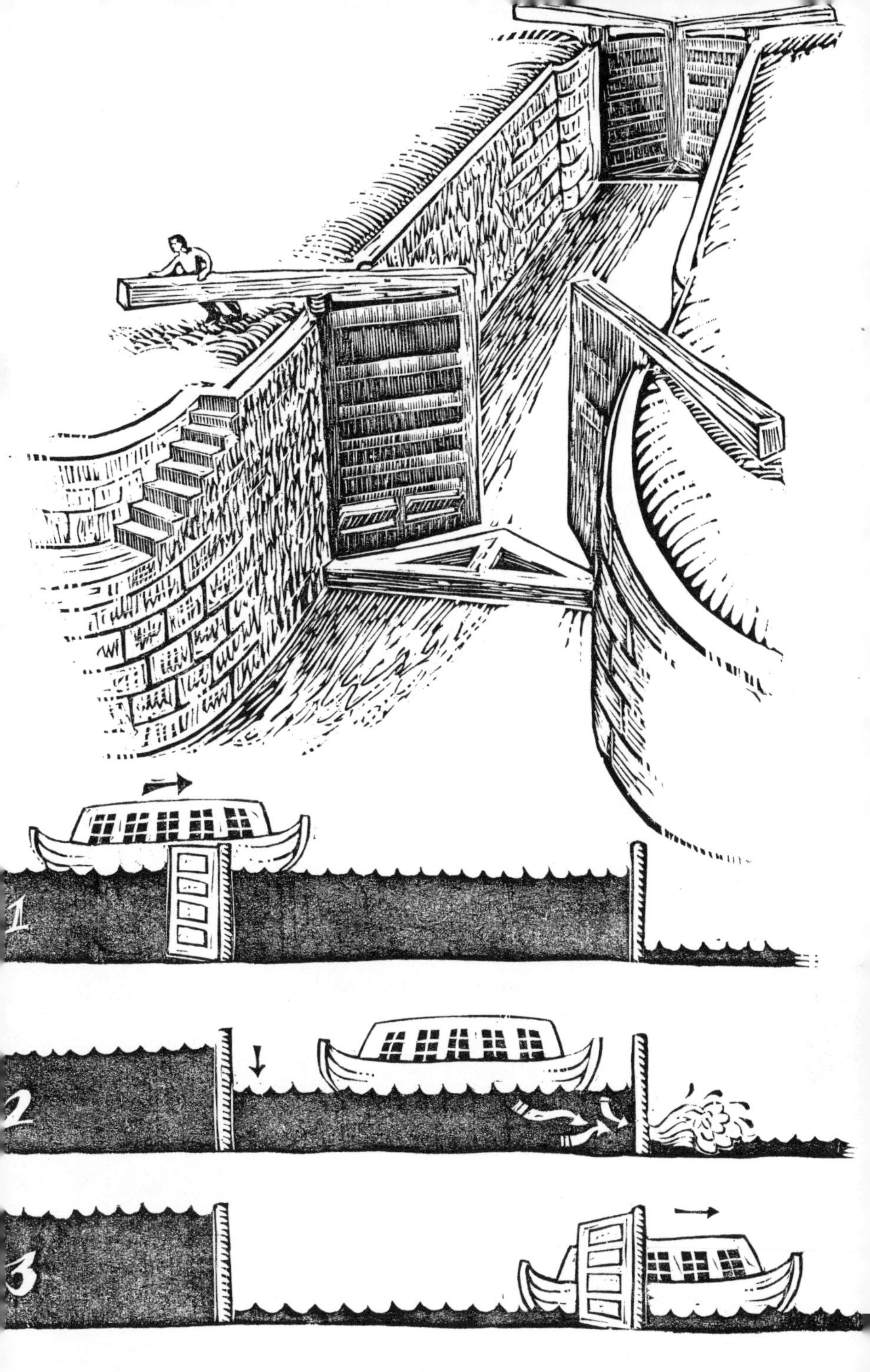
1
2
3

waterway across the width of the state—why that would take at least fifty years, maybe more.

Despite the rugged conditions of travel, De Witt Clinton finds this a stimulating experience. His curiosity as a natural scientist is aroused. Both the land and water are full of wondrous sights. He fills page after page in his diary with notes on wild flowers, birds, animals, and fish. The entry for July 9 includes this comment: "There is also an abundance of Mandrake or Wild-lemon, a delicious fruit as large as a Love-apple. . . . It is a plant, not a shrub."

On July 12 the party reaches Rome. Here a decision has to be made; it is just west of this village that the proposed routes separate. Morris and Van Rensselaer choose to go directly to Lake Erie by stagecoach while the other members plan to inspect the route that a canal to Lake Ontario would be expected to take.

It's a torturous trip to the shore of Lake Ontario, but these dedicated men are not to be deterred. After surveying all possibilities carefully, Clinton and his fellow travelers turn south and go back to the suggested route for a canal directly across the state to Lake Erie.

Not until August 3 do the five commissioners and Geddes reach Black Rock where Morris, Van Rensselaer, and their host, Peter B. Porter, are waiting. The trip has taken a month, under the most grueling conditions. But the commissioners have gained personal insight into the need for a canal. They understand now—as they never would have otherwise—what those who migrate west must endure, why so few ever dare try the trip.

After a sightseeing tour of Niagara Falls, the men return to Black Rock. Notes in hand, they discuss the advantages and disadvantages of both routes. Clinton is convinced that the canal must take the overland route, running directly across the state from Albany to Lake Erie. He insists that boats could be raised and lowered by locks, where necessary. Peter Porter opposes this idea vigorously. He wants a canal that will lead directly to Lake Ontario, using lakes and rivers wherever possible. This, he says, would eliminate much construction of an artificial waterway.

But, argues Clinton, there are definite objections. Both cargo and passengers would have to be transferred from canalboat to lake boat—back and forth—at the various ports along the way. Furthermore there's a danger that too much trade would be diverted to Canada if the Lake Ontario route were accepted. He is adamant that only one continuous canal within New York State will ever open up the western lands.

When the commissioners return to Albany, more meetings are held throughout the fall. Gouverneur Morris wants the overland canal but believes it should be built to slope gently downhill all the way from Lake Erie to Utica. Other members object, saying that is far too impractical, since it would necessitate building great embankments to carry the boats over the low areas. De Witt Clinton continues to plead for a canal with locks. In their final report the commissioners note that the artificial waterway *is* a practical venture, although the various issues about how it should be constructed are enumerated.

The following spring, on March 2, 1811, the report is presented to the state legislature. One month later, Clinton introduces a bill recommending that the commission continue its work and try to get sponsorship from the national government. The legislation is quickly passed; Clinton and Morris are chosen to go to Washington City and present the request to President James Madison.

Meanwhile, however, trouble is brewing with Great Britain. That country and France have been at war for the past eight years. His Majesty's ships now rule the seas, though finding crewmen for those ships has become a problem. Because of poor pay and miserable living conditions, hundreds of Englishmen have deserted from the British navy and found work on United States ships.

The British government has begun to claim the right to stop neutral ships in mid-ocean, remove sailors of British birth, and force or "impress" them back into the royal navy. Few members of the ships' crews have papers to prove their nationality. As a result, American seamen as well as British have been seized. Demands for retaliation to such high-handed tactics are being voiced all over this country.

On December 21, 1811, De Witt Clinton and Gouverneur Morris call at the President's House in Washington City. Mr. Madison receives them coldly. Despite Clinton's eloquent pleas for federal assistance in building the canal, the President refuses to lend his support to the project. There's no time now to think of internal improvements, he says. Just last month he warned Congress to get ready for war.

Regardless of the President's pessimism, the canal commission continues meeting throughout the spring of 1812. Then on June 18 a declaration of war is placed before Congress. It passes the Senate by a mere *six* votes. The nation now plunges once again into conflict with Great Britain.

For the present, all hope has been shattered for the construction of "Clinton's Ditch"—the nickname its opponents have given to the proposed canal.

CHAPTER 3

Tension and Triumph

1815–1817

As long as the war continues, nothing specific can be accomplished concerning the canal. Nevertheless the commissioners meet regularly and plan for the time when their efforts can be renewed. Then comes the news they have eagerly awaited. The Treaty of Ghent, ending the war, reaches President Madison on February 14, 1815; three days later it is formally ratified by the United States Senate.

Now the commission can go into action. Though the money allotted by the state legislature has been withdrawn to pay war debts, there must be other ways to secure the necessary funds. For the next nine months the men plot their strategy for reopening the canal issue.

Although the conflict with Great Britain has been

responsible for postponement of the artificial waterway, it is now evident that the War of 1812 has given new impetus to the project. Moving men and war materials from east to west was a costly process. A piece of ordnance worth four hundred dollars at the foundry cost the government two thousand dollars by the time it was delivered on the fighting line. The military effort was seriously restricted by the lack of good transportation. There were disastrous delays caused by the breakdown of wagons, the wearing out of horses.

On the night of December 30, 1815, a huge rally, sponsored by the commissioners, is held at City Hall in New York City. Both friends and enemies of the project are present. As mayor, De Witt Clinton's presence dominates the meeting. In a short speech he points out that the war has been over for almost a year. There are countless opportunities for increased trade awaiting. But only a waterway west can provide these opportunities. Drastic action must be taken!

Jonas Platt urges the preparation of a paper, a "memorial," to present to the state legislature. It should be, he says, so framed that it will convince the lawmakers they must authorize immediate construction of the canal. De Witt Clinton is named to draw up the memorial.

For the next few weeks Clinton devotes every spare moment to the task. In his study at Richmond

Hall, the house he owns in Greenwich Village, Clinton translates his visions into bold and exciting words. Goose quill in hand, he pens reasons why national growth is not only important but imperative; how such a canal "would perhaps convey more riches on its waters than any other canal in the world." He describes where the waterway should be built; how it is to be constructed with sixty-two locks—yes, sixty-two—that will make up for the changes in water levels through which the canal will pass. The probable cost he estimates at some six million dollars. In conclusion, he states:

It may be confidently asserted, that this canal, as to the extent of its route, as to the countries which it connects, and as to the consequences which it will produce, is without a parallel in the history of mankind. . . . It remains for a free state to create a new era in history, and to erect a work more stupendous, more magnificent, and more beneficial than has hitherto been achieved by the human race.

A thousand copies of this impressive seven thousand word document are printed and distributed to influential people throughout the state—newspaper editors, teachers, leading citizens, politicians, clergymen. Suddenly the canal issue has become very much alive. Enthusiastic supporters stage noisy rallies; mass meetings are held all over the state of New York. More than one hundred thousand people sign petitions endorsing the project.

There is also much opposition. Self-interest and jealousy cause persuasive politicians in New York City to denounce the canal; they accuse Clinton of using the canal project to further his own political ambitions, so that in future elections his popularity with the voting public will be assured. Wealthy farmers on Long Island and those who reside along the Hudson River fear competition from the west. People living in the southern counties near the Pennsylvania border are loud in their disapproval. They say they will have to help pay for a waterway they will never use.

Early in April 1816, De Witt Clinton takes the memorial and accompanying petitions to Albany and places them before a joint session of the legislature. He makes an impassioned plea for immediate action; certainly the lawmakers cannot disregard wishes of so large a number of voters.

On April 12, the state assembly approves a bill stipulating that construction shall begin on the middle section of the canal—from Rome to the Seneca River—the cost not to exceed two million dollars. This is not the all-inclusive legislation that the commissioners had hoped for, but at least it is a beginning.

When the bill comes before the state senate, Martin

Lake Ontario
Lockport
Rochester
Black Rock
Buffalo
Montezuma Swamps
Lake Erie
DE WITT CLINTON

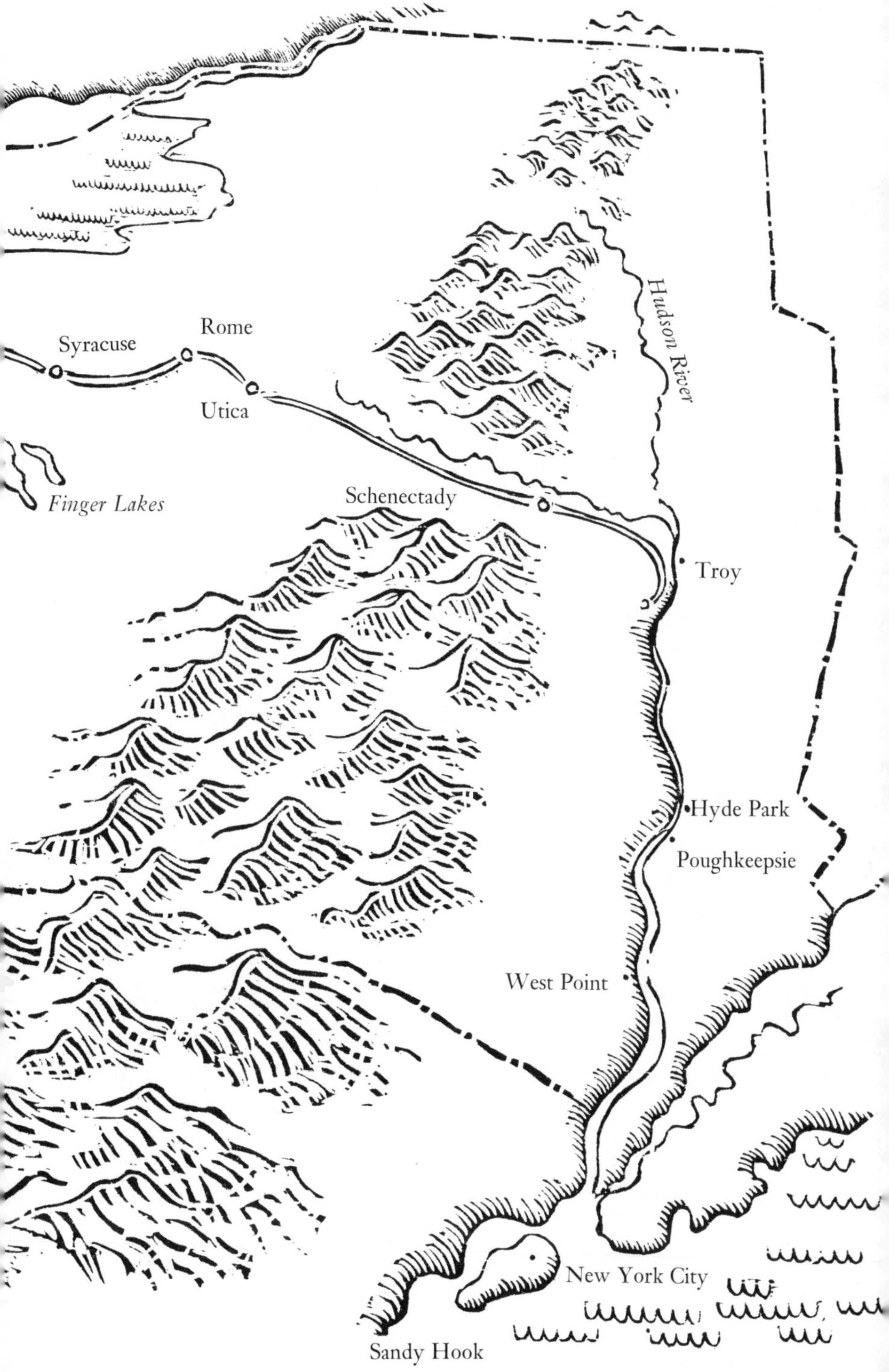

Syracuse
Rome
Utica
Hudson River
Finger Lakes
Schenectady
Troy
Hyde Park
Poughkeepsie
West Point
New York City
Sandy Hook

Van Buren, leader of the opposition forces, probes further into the details. It is evident, he says, that the precise line of the canal has not yet been staked out. Accurate surveys of the entire route should be made before any construction is started.

More debate follows. At last, on April 17, the amended legislation is passed, authorizing twenty thousand dollars for further surveys. A new five-member commission is appointed: De Witt Clinton will be chairman together with Stephen Van Rensselaer, Joseph Ellicott, Samuel Young, and Myron Holley.

For the pro-canal advocates, the delay is obviously a disappointment. Nevertheless the new commissioners waste no time setting to work. It is decided to divide the route into three sections. Charles C. Brodhead is to survey the eastern section, from Rome to the Hudson River. Benjamin Wright will supervise the middle section from the Seneca River to Rome, while James Geddes takes over the western section—from the Seneca River west to Lake Erie.

The five commissioners spend the summer traveling back and forth along the proposed channel. They watch the surveyors measuring each foot of the 363 miles; they study construction costs and come up with detailed estimates.

When Chairman Clinton returns in late August, he writes a friend:

We have looked at all the difficult points, ascended the mountains, penetrated the forests, descended into wide-speading and deeply excavated ravines and have encountered more fatigue than I thought I could bear. The result is most satisfactory. The work can be easily effected, and the utmost cost will not exceed our calculations. The public sentiment is also fixed in our favor. There is scarcely a dissentient in this vast country.

Now the canal issue is very much before the public. Clinton's rivals take this opportunity to deride him, possibly even destroy his political future. They magnify the dangers of digging such a waterway. They deplore the cost, hinting that the figures have been doctored to commit the state to the project.

To combat this dissension, De Witt Clinton spends many hours during the fall of 1816 writing letters to newspapers across the state. Using the pen name "Atticus," he paints glorious word pictures of what a canal can do for New York. There are tremendous trade possibilities; the state can become the instrument for opening up the west. He implores the people of New York State to cease their opposition. The canal, he writes, is "a child of the people . . . an object of such magnitude that the blind may see it." And he prophesies that "New York City will stand unrivalled by any city on the face of the earth."

Late in February 1817, Chairman Clinton presents the completed commission report to the legislature. On March 18 pro-canal lawmakers introduce a bill to begin construction of the artificial waterway. For almost a month the legislators argue the pros and cons.

Tension mounts as the days pass. Time is growing short; the legislature must soon adjourn for the year. Finally, on April 15, 1817, authorization is approved by both the assembly and the senate.

Oddly enough, it is Martin Van Buren who turns the tide in the senate. Though last year he violently opposed the canal, he has watched public enthusiasm grow. Prudent in the ways of politics, Van Buren realizes what is taking place throughout the state and declares he is in favor of the bill.

De Witt Clinton is jubilant. One final hurdle remains, however. According to the legislative rules of the state of New York, no bill can become law until approved by the Council of Revisions, a five-member body with absolute veto power.

The council convenes immediately. It is well known that two of its members are violently opposed to the measure—Chief Justice Smith Thompson and Acting Governor John Taylor. (Taylor became the chief executive earlier this spring when Governor Daniel Tompkins went to Washington City as Vice-President of the United States.) Jonas Platt and Joseph Yates favor the bill. The deciding vote will be cast by Chancellor James Kent, who sees interesting possibilities in a canal but says that it is too gigantic a project to be undertaken at this time.

Arguments now fly back and forth. For Jonas Platt, in particular, this is an important moment. It's been more than seven years since he persuaded De Witt Clinton to participate in the project. Will all the work of the canal commissioners go for nothing? Council members are interrupted in their debate by the unexpected appearance of Vice-President Tompkins, the former governor.

Though no one has asked Tompkins for his opinion, he cannot resist the opportunity to voice his opposition. "The late peace with Great Britain was a mere truce and," he predicts, "we shall undoubtedly soon have a renewal of war with that country. Instead of wasting the credit and resources of the State in this chimerical project, we ought immediately to employ all the revenue and credit of the State in providing arsenals, arming the militia, erecting fortifications and preparing for war."

Chancellor Kent is aghast. Though opposed to the canal, he is even more opposed to war. "Do you really think so, sir?" he questions Tompkins.

"Yes, sir!" replies the Vice-President, reminding his audience of Admiral Perry's triumph on Lake Erie. "England will never forgive us our victories on land, and on the ocean and the lake. And my word for it, we shall have another war within two years!"

Kent springs to his feet, his face grim with determination. "Gentlemen," he declares, "if we must have war or have a canal, I am in favor of the canal, and I vote for the canal."

Outside the statehouse, a violent April storm has been raging. But the gusty winds and drenching rain are no deterrent to the hundreds of people waiting to hear the verdict. Platt goes to the window and calls out to the crowd, "The bill has passed."

Shouts, cheers, huzzas, ring out. Strangers standing side by side clap each other on the shoulder in their excitement. At last—after so many years of planning and working—the Erie Canal is to be started!

CHAPTER 4

Digging Begins
1817

Authorization for construction of the canal in this spring of 1817 has an important political effect for De Witt Clinton. Nominated for the governorship of New York, he is elected by an overwhelming majority, the largest ever recorded in the state. Thus, in voting for Clinton, the people have also been expressing their approval of the waterway project.

Newsmen across the state are enthused about the canal. On May 15, 1817, the editor of the Albany *Gazette and General Advertiser* writes in a triumphant mood:

We believe the commencement of this splendid project will be hailed by the great body of the people of this state, as the dawning of an era which will be productive of more durable renown and glory to New York, than has been imparted to her by anything she has accomplished since the first settlement of the country.

Spearheaded by Governor Clinton, the canal commission wastes no time in getting plans underway. There are many, many decisions to be made. What should the overall width of the channel be? How deep? Because canalboats have neither oars nor sails, they will have to be pulled through the water by teams of animals—horses, mules, or oxen—walking alongside the canal on a towpath. How far above the water should the towpath be? How wide? These and hundreds of other problems must be solved before even the first shovelful of earth can be turned.

After the answers have been found, there are contracts that must be awarded for the middle section of the waterway. Since labor is scarce in this sparsely settled country, the commissioners hope that farmers along the proposed route will contract for the work and use their hired hands to do the digging. Thus construction will provide not only extra work but added income for the region's inhabitants.

It is decided that persons who want the job of contractor should submit sealed bids. The contractors must agree to dig a specific length of channel—anything from forty rods up to three miles—at a stated price. Successful bidders will then promise to house the men. Workers will be supplied with shovels, scrapers, teams of horses, and other essential equipment. Included in the rations and pay of each laborer will be a daily quota of whiskey.

Meanwhile, though the route has been established, James Geddes and Benjamin Wright search for the best place to start digging. They look for a long level stretch of land where the earth is soft and can be easily moved. Their test borings reveal that the Rome area is their answer. East and west from this spot, there are ninety-four miles of nearly flat terrain—between the Seneca and the Mohawk rivers. An adequate water supply is a necessity; certainly the Mohawk offers this.

People in Albany clamor that work on the canal should start in their town. It's only logical, they say; boats coming up the Hudson could float right into the canal. Admittedly from a political point of view, this might be a wise move. But the commissioners are not interested in politics right now. Rock would have to be blasted out and locks constructed, if the canal were begun at the Hudson River end. There are too many engineering problems to be solved where the land is not level. That can come later.

What's more, Governor Clinton points out to his fellow commissioners, progress in the middle section should be fairly rapid. It's most important, he adds, to have something completed as soon as possible—important both physically and psychologically. Once the canalboats start operating, all New Yorkers will realize what the waterway can mean to their state. Those living in the eastern and western sections of the route will also be anxious to enjoy the advantages of the canal. Undoubtedly they will bring pressure to bear on their state senators and representatives. And the legislature will be compelled to make appropriations adequate to complete the other two sections.

There's another consideration. Benjamin Wright has already agreed to superintend construction on the middle section. Since Rome is his home, he knows both the people and the countryside well. In fact, he's been surveying land around here for years.

On June 6, 1817, sealed bids are received by the commission. The first contract for the middle section is awarded to Judge John Richardson. Now arrangements must be made for a ceremony that will signal the beginning of construction. When is the most appropriate time?

Governor Clinton suggests that there is no more significant date to all America than the anniversary of the Declaration of Independence. Why not hold the opening ceremonies on the Fourth of July? he asks. That date might prove a good omen for the success of the canal. The other commissioners concur; the mayor of Rome, Judge Joshua Hathaway, is promptly notified of the commission's intent.

No news could have made the Rome villagers happier. To know that after years of waiting, of dreaming about what the waterway could mean to them—now it is about to happen. The people are overjoyed to think that their little wilderness settlement is to have the honor of conducting the opening ceremony for such an important occasion.

Volunteers begin work at once, clearing a small area in the forest near the edge of the proposed channel. Huge tree trunks are split in half and placed in rows—flat side up—to form a rough platform. Whale-oil torches are hung from the limbs of surrounding trees to add a festive note.

July 4, 1817, dawns bright and clear. Soon after sunrise most of Rome's seven hundred inhabitants are on hand for the spectacle, many of them armed with spades and shovels. Town officials and visiting dignitaries, impressive in their black frock coats and tall silk hats, form a procession and move out to the clearing.

An ear-spliting boom of cannons greets their arrival. Judge Hathaway, as mayor, begins the ceremony with a brief salutation and asks Colonel Samuel Young, representing the canal commissioners, to address the crowd. The colonel responds by saying:

Fellow citizens, we have assembled to commence the excavation of the Erie Canal. The work when accomplished will connect our western inland seas with the Atlantic Ocean. It will diffuse the benefits of internal navigation over a surface of vast extent, blessed with a salubrious climate and luxuriant soil, embracing a tract of country capable of sustaining more human beings than were accommodated by any work of the kind.

By this great highway, unborn millions will easily transport their surplus productions to the shores of the Atlantic, procure their supplies, and hold a useful and profitable intercourse with all the maritime nations of the earth.

The expense and labour of this great undertaking, bears no proportion to its utility. Nature has kindly afforded every facility; we have all the moral and physical means within our reach and control. Let us then proceed to the work, *animated by the prospect of its speedy accomplishment, and cheered with the anticipated benedictions of a grateful posterity.*

Now the dignitaries move off the platform and down to the channel markings. Mayor Hathaway hands a ceremonial spade to Colonel Young. He, in turn, passes it along to the first contractor, Judge John Richardson.

Someone in the crowd shouts, "Left foot first for luck!" as the judge steps forward on his left foot. He plunges the spade into the sod and lifts up the initial mound of earth. Cheers and huzzas fill the air. Cannon explode with a roar. Villagers who have brought shovels rush to the markings, eager to take part in this first day's digging. America's biggest construction project has just begun!

On the morning after the celebration the crews of local laborers, hired by Judge Richardson, arrive at the site. The right of way for the canal must be marked off by five rows of surveyors' red stakes, explains Superintendent Benjamin Wright. The outer two rows will be set sixty feet apart—this to indicate the outer edge of land to be cleared. The inner two rows, forty feet apart, will be the precise width of the canal. The fifth row should be placed in the exact center of the channel.

Fanning out east and west, the surveying crews begin their measurements, followed by workmen pounding in the stakes. It has been decided that only the necessary sixty feet will be cleared; this will save both time and money. Soon the laborers find themselves working in near darkness, so dense are the forests.

Next come the borers, testing the soil to a depth of twelve feet. It's essential to learn the kind of earth with which the men will be working. When problems arise, the engineers will have a better idea how to solve them, knowing the nature of the soil.

Behind the borers are the levelers and diggers. This is the most difficult job of all. Mile after mile of trees must be cut down; many are seven to eight feet in diameter. Once the trees have been burned and the land cleared, the digging begins.

Beneath the top soil is a dense mass of undergrowth —sturdy roots that have become twisted and tangled through the centuries. Grubbing out these roots is backbreaking work. Nevertheless the men are determined that nothing will stop them, now that construction has actually begun.

By mid-autumn, problems are beginning to pile up. Never in the history of the world has such a lengthy canal been attempted. As superintendent of the middle section, Benjamin Wright feels the need for more knowledge. One of his assistants, Canvass White, seems to have an uncanny ability in the field of mechanics. A native New Yorker, having been born and reared in Oneida County, he's already proved his skill in the work he has done thus far.

The superintendent decides to ask the young man to go to Europe so that White can inspect the canal systems there. By way of background, Wright explains that even before the birth of Christ, the Egyptians had built canals measuring as much as 125 miles

in length, though always on level land. The Romans followed their example but added aqueducts and tunnels. Then for centuries the art of canal building was lost. In the seventeenth century, Italian engineers revived the concept of canals; locks, devised in 1481, were used extensively by them. The Dutch, also, constructed hundreds of miles of artificial waterways.

Take a look at the Languedoc Canal that cuts across southern France, Wright suggests. It's been in existence more than one hundred and twenty-five years. Its one hundred and forty-four mile length, is well worth inspection, especially the one hundred and nineteen locks and its complex array of tunnels and aqueducts.

The British, too, have been great canal builders, Wright continues. Concentrate your efforts in England and Scotland. See how they have surmounted their problems. Furthermore the superintendent suggests that White buy some modern surveying instruments and take notes on anything that may be helpful to the Erie.

Elated by his assignment, Canvass White makes arrangements to leave immediately. He equips himself with a satchel full of maps and several pairs of sturdy walking shoes. Then the young man books passage for Europe, filled with determination to find out everything possible for the success of the New York canal.

Throughout the fall months there is no break in the intensity of work. Even after the snow begins to fly, the laborers continue hacking their way through the forest, shoveling to a depth of four feet for the actual path of the forty-foot wide channel.

Alongside the canal there's the towpath to be constructed, a pathway, ten feet in width, where the animals will walk as they pull the boats through the water. On the opposite side of the towpath is a narrow ledge called the *berm*, which is suitable for pedestrians. Building up the embankments to hold both paths requires great physical stamina. Yet no one complains.

By the end of December 1817, when cold weather brings construction to a halt, approximately fifteen miles of the canal have been completed. Fifty-eight miles more are under contract. All this has been accomplished with barely six months of work. Surely those who have scoffed at the idea of a canal will now be silenced—or will they?

CHAPTER 5

Solving the Problems

1818

Once the frozen ground has begun to thaw in the early spring of 1818, work is resumed on the canal. When problems mount up, Yankee ingenuity takes over. Several workmen come forward with new ways to speed up the seemingly endless task of clearing out the area.

One of the first of these is the invention of one of the contractors, Jeremiah Brainard of Rome. The conventional wheelbarrow has proved to be an awkward device for loading and unloading dirt. Brainard takes a single flexible board and bends it into a semicircular shape. Thus the bottom and sides are all one piece. It's more durable, much lighter to transport, and far easier to unload.

Felling the forest trees is a time-consuming job, one that requires several men with axes, chopping away at the sturdy trunks hour after hour. An ingenious worker suddenly has an idea. He climbs to the top of one of the trees and secures a heavy cable. Back on the ground he takes the other end of the cable and drags it out about one hundred feet from the base of the tree. There he attaches it to a large wheel worked by an endless-screw gear. Slowly, very slowly, he winds the gear with a crank, exerting such pressure that irresistible force topples the tree. Now one man can do the work of several—and in much less time.

Pulling out tree stumps is a tedious procedure, complicated by the angle of stubborn roots which must be extracted from the earth. Valuable time is lost as workmen struggle with the exasperating underground growth. Again Yankee ingenuity comes to the forefront.

One group of laborers rigs up a machine they call a "stump puller." It's a thirty-foot-long axle, supported by two wheels that are sixteen feet in diameter. A chain is wound around the center of the axle and fastened to the stump. Sturdy rope coiled on a third wheel is attached to a team of oxen. After the machine is secured, the oxen pull on the rope, which in turn tightens the chain and pulls out the stump within minutes. Seven men are required to operate the device, but even so, thirty or forty stumps can be extracted and hauled away in a day.

Now another problem arises to plague the builders. The channel being dug is forty feet wide, but the sides are slanted, and at the bottom, it's only twenty-eight feet in width. In some places, however, the earth is too sandy, and the slanted sides begin to crumble. There's more improvising, more experimenting. Then one day several workers discover a stiff clay in one of the adjoining fields; "the blue mud of the meadows," they call it. By using this clay as a lining for the sides, the banks remain firm, and water seepage is eliminated.

In mid-March, Canvass White returns from his trip abroad. He reports to Benjamin Wright that he has walked two thousand miles along the towpaths of England and Scotland, inspecting every aspect of canal building. He's made detailed sketches of locks and taken innumerable notes on the construction methods used by the British. He's also brought back the newest instruments for measuring and testing.

But, White adds, there is something even more important. During his tour he met an Irishman, J. J. McShane, who is a splendid canal-construction engineer. Currently he is engaged as a maintenance man for three of England's longest canals. White has persuaded him to come to New York late this spring and bring his experienced crew of workmen with him. They have all promised to take jobs on the Erie.

"Splendid!" says Wright, complimenting the young man on the thoroughness with which he has completed the overseas assignment. Meanwhile there is a new crisis—one so serious that it may bring the entire project to an end unless an answer can be found.

The problem concerns the canal locks, Wright explains. Those built with wooden blocks are already deteriorating. It's imperative to use cement to hold these blocks firm, but there's only one kind that will harden underwater—that's hydraulic cement. And there's no source of hydraulic cement in this country. England has it, but transporting the immense quantity needed across the ocean and trekking it back into the wilderness country poses an impossible situation. The expense would be staggering, probably enough to bankrupt the project.

Seeing the look of despair on the superintendent's face, Canvass White promises to start searching for a way to solve this dilemma. He's certain he can find an answer.

During the next few days White rides along the canal route, scrutinizing various fragments of stone. Near Chittenango in Madison County, he discovers a limestone deposit that interests him. Chipping out some of the limestone, White drops it into his saddlebag and stops at a nearby tavern to spend the night.

There he does some experimenting. First he burns the limestone, then pulverizes it. Adding sand and water to make it pliable, White rolls the small mass into a ball and drops it into a bucket of water.

Peering into the bucket the following morning, the young man is amazed to find that overnight the mass has turned to a ball of stone. Canvass White is overjoyed! Here is the answer. This is "water-proof lime" that will work as well as—maybe even better than—imported hydraulic cement.

Though the crisis of finding a suitable cement has been solved, Benjamin Wright is now faced with a new problem. The farmers who have been hired as contractors consider their jobs a mere sideline. Some are very efficient; others are far too slow. There's no consistency in the progress of the various crews. Besides, when crops must be planted or harvested, these contractors take their men off the canal to do the necessary farm work. What is needed is a force of several thousand laborers who will report day after day, week after week—men who will devote their entire time to constructing the waterway.

Again Wright consults Canvass White. Where in the world will they find enough laborers to do the necessary front-line digging? He's already tried some freed slaves who had come north looking for jobs. But most of them disliked the work and soon quit. In this thinly populated state, adds Wright, shaking his head, there just aren't enough men interested in such backbreaking activity.

White agrees that this is a serious problem. Perhaps there is an answer, though. He recalls several conversations with J. J. McShane, the Irishman who has agreed to come to New York and work on the Erie. McShane told White that the native Irish are willing and dependable as laborers. Why not start a campaign to interest them?

The superintendent nods. It's certainly worth a try, he says. Everyone knows there's been a mass migration of the Irish to America. Some say as many as ten thousand are coming each year, but most of them have settled in the cities. Why not circulate word that brawny young Irishmen will be welcomed on the canal crews?

White promises to start the campaign immediately. Even better, he'll employ recruiters to meet the immigrant ships coming into New York City. These Irish laborers can be hired as soon as they set foot in this country.

Within a week White's agents are on the piers, waiting for the vessels from Ireland to dock. As the newcomers stream down the gangplank, the men are approached and asked if they would like jobs digging a canal in upstate New York.

The pay will be "fifty cents and found"—"found" being board and lodging, the recruiters explain. Further, it's fifty cents a day, not a week. To the unskilled workmen who in Ireland have been earning not more than a dime a day, this sounds like a small fortune. Hundreds accept the proposition and are transported up the Hudson River in small sloops. From Albany teams of wagons take them out to the middle section of the waterway.

The Irishmen soon discover that life on the construction site is not easy. The hours are long, the work strenuous. The men are housed in wooden shacks thrown up by the contractors. Two tiers of wooden bunks line the four walls. A pine plank is the only mattress, unless the occupant brings his own bedding, and few do. Windows are square openings without glass or screens; the mosquitoes swarm in during the hot weather, interrupting the sleep of the tired workers.

Half an hour before sunrise each morning, the cook's helper blasts the wake-up horn. "All out. Mush in the kettle," he shouts. Breakfast is hearty. Usually there are fried eggs, sausage or pork chops, steak, ham, potatoes, corn bread, batter cakes with molasses, and fried mush. To wash down the food, there is a choice of skimmagig (buttermilk), fresh milk, tea, or coffee.

While the Irishmen stow away the food, the kitchen crew packs the quart-size dinner pails to be carried out to the work area. Then comes the call, "Pick and shovel!" and the crew trudges off to work. Those who loiter behind are threatened with a fine for being late.

By the time the sun comes up, everyone is busy.

Axmen clear out the underbrush. Teamsters hitch up their oxen to the fallen tree trunks and haul them away. Shovelers toss up great mounds of earth while supervisors make certain the diggers are going down deep enough.

There's a half-hour break at noon when the camp cook brings out a ten-gallon kettle of steaming coffee and the workers rush for their dinner pails. By eating hastily, there's still time enough to smoke a pipe or enjoy a pinch of snuff. Then it's back to the various jobs until sunset. During the long summer days, work sometimes lasts twelve or fourteen hours.

"Grog time" is a welcome institution. At certain intervals during the day a young boy, called a "jigger boss," carries rations of whiskey up and down the line; the workmen look forward to this refreshment.

By nightfall everyone is ready for a big supper. At first, game from the nearby forests—squirrel, partridge, bear, and venison—is the staple fare. After several months, however, the laborers revolt. They demand beef and pork. The contractors have to promise to vary the menu; they agree to serve game only on specified days.

Most of the Irishmen have been farmers and field hands in their native country; now they face the challenge of making good in this new land. After the men become more accustomed to the heavy work, a comradeship develops among the construction crews.

The men begin singing while they heave their shovels and pickaxes, singing a song that they themselves made up:

> "*We are cutting a Ditch through the gravel,*
> *Through the gravel across the state, by heck!*
> *We are cutting the Ditch through the gravel,*
> *So the people and the freight can travel,*
> *Can travel across the state, by heck!*"

Rivalry develops as the immigrants work alongside the Americans. Speed increases; the pace picks up. Benjamin Wright wonders what he would have done if the Irish laborers hadn't come to his rescue.

CHAPTER 6

Near Disaster and New Waters

1819

In the early spring of 1819, the commissioners are pleased with the progress on the middle section of the canal. One threat, however, remains—the forbidding Montezuma swamps, west of Syracuse.

Canvass White goes out to investigate conditions in the marshy area. He returns with the report that it's grim country, filled with dense thickets of tall reeds growing in oozing black muck. In fact, he says, it's neither land nor water but "a streaky unpleasant mixture of both." The Cayuga Indians have also warned him that "a great sickness" will come to anyone attempting to invade this wasteland. Nevertheless the canal line must run four and a half miles across the swamps. If the Erie is ever to be completed, work cannot stop here.

When work crews are first sent into the area, the men find it easy in this mire to dig out the channel. There is no rock to chisel, no tree stumps to remove. They laugh about how quickly they can build up the embankments alongside the channel. When work ceases at sunset, they've completed a good firm wall. Unfortunately it dissolves overnight as the mud slides back into the channel.

To combat this problem, the worried contractors decide to erect a crude retaining wall. Work is delayed while woodsmen are dispatched to the nearest forest to cut down trees and saw out the necessary pieces. After the wood is hauled back to the swamps, part of the crew begins driving stakes through the muck into the solid clay beneath. Planks are nailed across the stakes to hold up the embankment. This proves satisfactory except in certain places where the stakes slip through the ground and disappear. Quicksand is something everyone fears.

Working conditions here in the Montezuma swamps are far from pleasant. The men stand for hours in water above their knees; their legs swell. Leeches attack them. But wages are good or "hire," as the men call it; and besides, there's more work waiting when these few miles are finished. So they turn their discomfort into a joke and nickname some of the worst places "Backbreak Bog," "Digger's Misery," "Bottomless Pit," and "Mudturtles' Delight." Singing

on the job lifts their spirits, and they compose another verse for the Canal Builders' Song:

"*We are digging the Ditch through the mire;*
Through the mud and the slime and the mire, by heck!
And the mud is our principal hire;
In our pants, up our sleeves, down our neck, by heck!
The mud is our principal hire."

In spite of all the unpleasantness, work continues to progress until mid-July when hordes of mosquitoes and gnats swarm into the marshes. Millions of the flying insects descend on the unsuspecting laborers. Their hands become so swollen they can scarcely hold the shovels; their eyes puff up until it's difficult to see. Sleep in the steaming shacks is impossible.

The contractors procure smudge buckets for the workers to hang around their necks—"Montezuma necklaces," someone names them. At the bottom of each bucket a tiny fire is lighted, covered with twigs and wet leaves. It is hoped that the rising smoke will drive away the gnats and mosquitoes. In some few instances the smudge buckets do bring relief, but most of the time the workers simply choke on the smoke. Red eyes and raw throats plague them.

Early in August the mosquitoes bring on a disastrous epidemic. More than a thousand men are stricken with fever and chills; many are too ill to leave their bunks. Courageous doctors go into the swamps to treat the patients—first by bleeding them and then administering snake-root, green pigweed, and something called "Seneca oil" (a medicine that is pure kerosene). Only Jesuits' bark seems to have any healing effects. Imported from Peru, the new drug contains a crude form of quinine.

Still there are hundreds of casualties. Someone starts a rumor the digging in the swamps has released fumes that will scatter poison throughout the surrounding countryside; innocent people, as well as workers, will be stricken. As word of the conditions spreads, laborers are thrown into a panic. Men who are well enough to walk desert the work camps in droves. Construction comes to a standstill.

The first frost of autumn brings new hope. The mosquitoes and the deadly disease disappear. Once again work resumes. Digging in half-frozen earth is easier than in the oozing slime. Contractors push doggedly ahead so that completion by next spring is assured. In some places it's necessary to build a wooden towpath supported on piles or pontoons to assure safe footing for the tow horses.

The near disaster in the Montezuma swamps has occasioned all sorts of wild rumors—New York will never get its artificial waterway; it will be impossible to finish the canal. Now the commissioners decide to open the completed fifteen-mile stretch of channel between Rome and Utica. Although an additional seventy-nine miles have been dug, that part will not be navigable before next summer. It is hoped to convince the public that progress has been made, that there really *is* a canal. A celebration is planned for mid-October.

One of the complexities of building an artificial waterway is how to provide it with water. In addition to the thousands of workmen digging the canal, hundreds more have been working several miles away. They have constructed an intricate system of feeder channels to conduct water from nearby rivers and streams into the canal itself. The flow will be controlled by sluice gate and waste gates, a flow sufficient to provide the necessary four-foot depth along the whole of the Erie Canal's 363-mile length.

Before the canal can be opened to traffic, it must be filled with water. The day prior to the big celebration is designated for the crucial test. Benjamin Wright, Canvass White, and their assistants gallop up and down the fifteen-mile towpath, watching anxiously as the sluice gates swing open. Slowly the water begins to trickle in . . . then faster and faster it flows. Will the embankments withstand the pressure? Will the towpath remain firm? No one knows; all they can do is wait.

Rodmen are stationed in mid-channel with their measuring sticks. One foot and rising . . . two feet

. . . three feet. Finally comes the triumphant shout, "Four feet and holding." The sluice gates are closed. A few small leaks develop, but these are quickly plugged by the repair gangs. The initial crisis for the Erie is past.

On the morning of October 23, 1819, excited spectators pour into the area from miles around, eager to witness the first voyage on the canal. The boat is a sixty-one-foot-long craft, especially built for this grand occasion and christened *Chief Engineer of Rome* in honor of Benjamin Wright. On deck a military band strikes up as the honored guests step aboard: Governor Clinton, his fellow commissioners, members of the state legislature, executive engineers, and leading citizens of the Rome–Utica region.

After the ceremonial speeches are finished, bells ring out and cannons boom to mark the important day. Crowds lining the banks shout and cheer as the *Chief* moves down the waterway, pulled by a single horse trudging along the towpath.

A newsman for the Rochester *Telegraph* records the dramatic moment for his readers:

To see the first boat launched, to be among the first that were borne on the waters of a canal which is to connect the great chain of western lakes with the Hudson, and which will be one of the most stu-

pendous works the world has ever known, produced emotions which those only who felt them can conceive.

In the rush and excitement of opening this first stretch of the canal, none of the commissioners has thought about regulations to govern the navigation. No toll has been established for the one lock near Rome; no rules have been made for the use of the towpath. People living alongside the canal look at the waterway as a fascinating new toy.

Farmers handy with hammers and saws build crude boats to give their families an evening's outing. If the craft springs a leak, no matter. Let it sink. It's easy to patch together another one tomorrow. Before many days pass, the canal is filled with "handmades"—canoes, dugouts, and bateaux. These soon prove to be a major irritation to the freight-boat captains attempting to transport cargo on the waterway.

Suddenly fishing becomes a favorite sport, too. Trout, bass, eel, pickerel, and perch float in through the feeder channels. The embankment is lined with men tossing out their lines for an easy catch. Some even wade into the four-foot depth to spear eel.

Enterprising landowners discover another use for the canal. Heretofore, moving timber from one part of the farm to another has been a major chore: chaining the logs, hitching up the oxen to drag the wood over bumpy terrain. Now they merely roll the wood into the water and wait for a strong breeze. Very convenient, the farmers agree.

The towpath also becomes clogged with traffic. People driving their carts from one village to another find it much smoother for travel than the corduroy roads through the forests. And who wants to pay toll on a bumpy turnpike, when this highway is free? After dark the sports-minded young men in the county like to bring out their horses for a race.

Before long the canalboat captains become infuriated by the obstacles in the water and along the towpath. The commissioners are besieged with bitter complaints. Was the Erie constructed for the diversion of the country people, or is it to be used for regularly scheduled passenger and freight travel? And what about all the discarded boats? Too many hulls have been damaged by plowing into the unseen craft.

After listening to the accusations, the canal commission sets up some regulations. No animals are to be allowed on the towpath except horses or oxen used to pull the boats. Fishing is prohibited. Any person leaving a sunken boat in the water will be fined ten dollars. If rubbish is dumped into the canal, a five-dollar penalty will be assessed. Unfortunately the rules are not strictly enforced; the commissioners don't want the canal project to become unpopular with the people of Oneida County.

In the initial stages of planning, one of the sources of revenue was to be the toll paid by each canalboat using the Erie. Now the commissioners become aware that they haven't yet established a toll rate. Once it is set, some canalboat captains try to evade the charge. They wrap the feet of their horses in soft cloths and attempt to slip by the toll collector after dark.

An ingenious collector at Rome devises a trap. He rigs up a network of iron chains which he lowers into the water at dusk. When a captain tries to edge his boat through the toll station, it is snagged by the chains. After several red-faced culprits are caught, word gets around. There's no more toll-dodging on the canal.

Though a surprising amount of construction on the waterway has been accomplished during this year of 1819, the people of New York State are becoming impatient. For those anxious to move west, it's difficult to realize that a waterway across the state will take several years to build.

Governor Clinton's political enemies are loud in their criticism. Clinton, they remind people, was swept into office on the promise that the project would be finished by 1823. Sneeringly they point out that after more than two years of work, only fifteen miles have been completed. Dire predictions are circulated that the crazy ditch will never be finished. The governor's popularity is rapidly declining.

CHAPTER 7

Progress and Politics

1820–1822

At the time that the fifteen-mile length of canal was opened in the Rome area last October, few of Governor Clinton's critics knew about the additional seventy-nine miles of the middle section that had already been dug. As soon as the ice begins to melt in this spring of 1820, work crews move in to complete this part of the waterway.

Anticipating the opening of the canal, a shipping company is formed. From a sketch that Canvass White brought back from England, a packet boat is built, seventy-six feet in length and fourteen feet in width. It's the first passenger-carrying boat on the canal and makes its initial voyage from Rome to Syracuse on April 21, 1820.

Early in June the craft begins regularly scheduled

trips between these two ports, a distance of some fifty miles. The time involved is usually from ten to eleven hours, depending upon how much traffic the captain encounters. The packet comfortably accommodates forty or forty-five passengers, though at times many more jam into the narrow boxlike cabin. The interior of the cabin is equipped with tables for dining, and bunks for overnight travel. At present, however, the trips are scheduled for daylight hours so travelers can climb to the upper deck and enjoy the passing panorama. Because there are no locks to negotiate, this particular stretch of the canal is known as "the long level." Fare is four dollars each way, including three meals. It's more expensive than traveling by stagecoach, but there are no complaints. The ride is so smooth, the scenery so fascinating.

With the middle section nearly completed, contractors and laborers alike redouble their work efforts. Before the end of the month, the ninety-six miles from Utica to Montezuma on the Seneca River are ready for navigation. The commissioners plan a celebration for July Fourth, precisely three years after the first shovelful of earth was turned at Rome. They hope to focus attention on their progress. Perhaps such a gala occasion will inspire everyone in New York State and the chances of completing the waterway will be improved.

As word of the celebration spreads, residents from

six counties work feverishly, decorating special floats and craft to participate in the big event. On the appointed day seventy-three boats assemble in the basin at Syracuse, while hundreds line the banks to watch the proceedings. Aboard the *Oneida Chief* is Governor Clinton along with several members of the legislature, the commissioners, and distinguished guests from the surrounding countryside.

Samuel Miles Hopkins delivers a lengthy address in which he praises "the prosperity of the American empire and the rising glory of the state of New York." Afterward, the long procession of boats moves through the newly opened waters, accompanied by whistles and shouts from the crowd. Never before has such a spectacle been witnessed in the interior of this state.

Despite the trouble in the Montezuma swampland, most of the construction has proceeded fairly smoothly, since the land along the middle section is level. But now, as the work crews move into the eastern and western sections, the engineers are confronted by new problems. The country is rough and hilly. There are turbulent rivers to be crossed; most of these lie in deep valleys, far lower than the line of the canal.

After much consultation, it is decided that the safest, most satisfactory solution will be to construct aqueducts high above the rivers and streams. An

aqueduct is a water-carrying bridge built on the same level with the canal, so that animals pulling the boat walk directly onto the bridge. Many aqueducts are of open stone-arch construction, though some are wooden boxlike structures, open at either end. Both types are erected on stone supports, strong enough to bear the weight of the four-foot depth of water, the towpath, and the boats with their passengers and cargo.

Wherever a farmer's acreage is split by the canal, the commissioners have promised to build an "occupation bridge," a bridge that will allow the landowner to cross from one part of his farm to the other. When the waterway has been completed, it's estimated there will be more than three hundred of these small spans. In order to economize, they are built very low, only seven and a half feet above the water.

With the middle section now open and the passenger packets operating, the steersman must always be on the alert. Whenever the craft approaches one of these spans, he shouts a warning: "Low Bridge! Everybody down!" Passengers on the upper deck must duck quickly to avoid being knocked over, or even worse, swept overboard and seriously injured.

Throughout this spring of 1820, the political situation has become more and more tense. The anti-canal men have persuaded Daniel D. Tompkins, the Vice-President of the United States, to return to his home state and oppose De Witt Clinton for the office of governor in the fall election. From the very beginning, Tompkins has been vocal in his opposition to the waterway.

The campaign is a bitter one. Clinton's supporters dwell on the fact that almost one hundred miles of the Erie are now open to traffic, that farmers in upstate New York are finding this new mode of transportation a faster, less expensive way to send their produce to market. There's also been a surge of passenger travel along the canal; upstaters enjoy boating from one town to another.

The governor's opponents, however, are quick to point out that the middle section is the easiest part to build. Now that construction has started on both east and west sections, there's plenty of trouble ahead. Expenses are already piling up. These detractors predict financial disaster. The state will go bankrupt . . . the canal will never be finished.

On Election Day some 180,000 citizens of the state of New York go to the polls to cast their ballots. De Witt Clinton retains his office, though he receives less than a 2,000–vote majority. Certainly this is not a large vote of confidence for the governor and his waterway. Nevertheless Clinton moves immediately for legislative authorization to finance completion of the east and west sections. The lawmakers battle for days, but finally the bill is approved.

Even though the money has been allocated, anti-Clinton forces begin plotting to halt progress on the canal. Many New York City merchants fear competition from the west. Ease of transportation will cause prices to fall and lower profits. They persuade their representatives in Albany to propose that work on the western section be stopped until the eastern section is completed. This delaying action, they argue, will induce the public to lose interest. In spite of much conniving behind closed doors, the scheme fails; the proposal is defeated.

Governor Clinton is convinced that above all else, he must be honest with the people of his state. For this reason he announces that progress has been slower than expected. The canal cannot be finished in 1823. There have been too many construction problems; the completion date must be extended to 1825. But by this time, he promises, all 363 miles will be open to traffic.

An outburst of criticism follows the governor's announcement. The canal will never be finished, scoff Clinton's enemies, not in the year 1825 or any other year. It's preposterous to even consider a waterway that runs the width of the state.

Nevertheless there are many who begin to wonder

about the derogatory remarks when the annual report of the canal commissioners is published in late December 1820. It reads:

The novelty of seeing large boats drawn by horses, upon waters artificially conducted—through cultivated fields, forests, and swamps, over ravines, creeks and morasses, and from one elevation to another, by means of ample, beautiful and substantial locks, has been eminently exhilarating. The precision of the levels, the solidity of the banks, the regularity of the curves, the symmetry of the numerous and massive stone works, the depth of excavation in some places, the extent of the embankments in others, and the impression produced everywhere along the line, by the visible effects of immense labor, have uniformly afforded gratification mingled with surprise.

Meanwhile a strong rivalry has developed between two tiny hamlets at the western edge of the state. Buffalo and Black Rock are mere trading posts now, but everyone knows that one of these villages will be chosen as the terminal point for the canal. The favored one will undoubtedly become an important port city, the other doomed to obscurity.

Whenever there's a rumor that Buffalo is the choice, the inhabitants celebrate by firing off a rusty old cannon, aimed in the direction of Black Rock, four and a half miles to the north. The rival villagers then rush over, fists clenched for a fight. In the riot that follows there are many bloodied noses and cracked heads.

If someone starts a story that the canal will terminate at Black Rock, their artillery is wheeled out, and Buffalo receives a blast. Another riot is inevitable between the warring factions. Only a decision by the canal commissioners can end this fierce rivalry, but thus far the members have been unable to make up their minds.

The year 1821 is a difficult one for De Witt Clinton. His political enemies and those who oppose the canal project have banded together under the leadership of Martin Van Buren. This powerful group, known as the Albany Regency, has managed to gain control of both the state assembly and senate. Every move Clinton makes is blocked. Filling the dual role of governor and canal commission chairman is not only difficult but time-consumming. Clinton's faith in the Erie Canal never falters, however. He spends as much time as possible riding out to inspect construction, encourage the workers, offer technical assistance when it's needed.

On January 2, 1822, the governor addresses a joint session of the state legislature. He describes the progress of the canal in glowing terms. He reports that Illinois and Ohio are already considering similar undertakings. And with a note of pride in his voice, he adds that those states have asked for his advice. At the conclusion of the speech, there is only a scattering of applause; most of the lawmakers remain silent.

Wise in the ways of politics, De Witt Clinton now recognizes that his popularity is fading, that the Albany Regency has the upper hand, at least for the present. Several months later he announces that he will not seek renomination as the governor of New York.

Clinton, however, is a fighter. He refuses to believe that one election signifies either success or defeat in a political career. Once this term is ended, he intends to devote all his time to the project dearest to his heart—the completion of the Erie Canal by 1825. As chairman of the commission, he will keep his promise to the people.

Throughout this frustrating year of 1822, the anti-canal factions have often quoted Thomas Jefferson as saying that "such a waterway will never become a reality." Late in December, Clinton is particularly gratified to receive a letter from the former President of the United States. Mr. Jefferson writes:

. . . New York has anticipated, by a full century, the ordinary progress of improvement. This great work suggests a question, both curious and difficult, as to the comparative capability of nations to execute

great enterprises. It is not from surplus of produce, after supplying their own wants, for in this New York is not beyond some other states; is it from other sources of industry additional to her produce? This may be—or is it a moral superiority? a sounder calculating mind, as to the most profitable employment of surplus, by improvement of capital, instead of useless consumption? I should lean to this latter hypothesis, were I disposed to puzzle myself with such investigations; but at the age of 80, it would be an idle labour, which I leave to the generation which is to see and feel its effect, and add therefore only, the assurance of my great esteem and respect,

Thomas Jefferson

CHAPTER 8

Challenge After Challenge

1823–1824

Enthusiasm for the canal is running high as the summer of 1823 approaches. Newspapers are filled with stories about the new waterway. On June 25 a reporter for the Rochester *Telegraph* writes:

On Wednesday last a boat was launched from the yard of H. Goodman & Co., and though we may not announce the event in as lofty language as is used in city prints on like occasions, yet perhaps it was an occurrence equally interesting as the launching of the proudest ship from a seaport. To behold a vessel committed to the water 400 miles inland, and in a place which ten years ago was a wilderness . . . excites emotions of no common kind.

Now more than eighteen hundred boats are operating along the canal for a distance of some 220 miles, operating so successfully that the commissioners find it necessary to establish a speed limit. Their order reads, "Henceforth, speeds of only four miles per hour will be permitted on the Erie Canal, necessary to discourage the breakneck velocity some are attempting, streaking along at what appears to be five miles an hour." A penalty of ten dollars will be imposed on those captains who exceed the authorized limit. It's been discovered that any faster speed produces waves that might damage the earthen banks of the canal.

One important decision still remains for the canal commission. Will the western terminal point of the canal be located at Black Rock or Buffalo? In the midsummer of 1823, the commissioners and five supervisors spend two weeks investigating the facilities of both communities. After careful surveys, they determine that the harbor at Buffalo has a higher water level than does Black Rock on the Niagara River. And this will greatly reduce the cost of excavation in digging the canal eastward. So the nod is given to Buffalo.

The excited villagers plan a big ground-breaking ceremony. All who own oxen are invited to bring them. On the morning of August 9 the people gather on a boggy flat near Buffalo. While a hastily organized band plays lively tunes, twelve yoke of oxen are hitched to a huge plow. At a blast from the village's rusty cannon, a long whip is cracked; the clumsy creatures move forward as the plow blade bites into the sod between the red stakes marking the canal line. So important is this celebration that everyone wants a part in it.

Though the people of Buffalo have spent three years trying to prove their readiness for the canal, no one has thought about how the broken earth will be removed. Suddenly they realize there's not a scraper or a wheelbarrow anywhere in this wilderness village.

The determined citizens refuse to be delayed by lack of equipment. Once again Yankee ingenuity comes to the rescue. Several men go into a nearby forest and devise a carrier which they nickname their "soul cart." Two ten-foot poles are hewn from tree limbs and placed in a parallel position. Nailed to the center of the poles is a crude platform upon which great piles of sod can be thrown. Hauling away debris on this cart requires only two men; so successful is the carrier that soon dozens of similar carts are in use. A local reporter writes that "everyone from judges to urchins pitched in" to help.

North of Buffalo, the level land rises sharply into a mountainous ridge, a ridge that continues eastward for seven miles, three miles of which are solid stone. Ever since the canal route was first determined, the commissioners have known that this particular area would be their greatest challenge. They decide that the only solution will be to carve a channel through the rock, one that must be twenty-seven feet wide and varying in depth from thirteen to thirty feet. In addition, a narrow towpath is to be chiseled out of the side rock. In some places horses and driver will be a dizzying sixty feet above the boat they are towing.

At the eastern edge of these rocky cliffs is the tiny outpost of Lockport. Here vessels going east will have to descend some sixty feet to the level of the countryside below before they can continue their journey. Crafts traveling west will someday have to ascend these same heights. But how is this to be accomplished?

For the past five years one of Benjamin Wright's assistants, Nathan S. Roberts, has been puzzling over the problem of getting the canal up this face of sheer rock. With only surveyor's instruments and a few reference books, he has finally submitted a daring design. It's just been approved by Governor Clinton and his fellow commissioners.

Roberts' spectacular plan calls for the construction of a double set of five locks—one side to accommodate the descending eastbound traffic, the other for ascending westbound craft. Each lock will have a lift of twelve feet rather than the usual eight feet, four

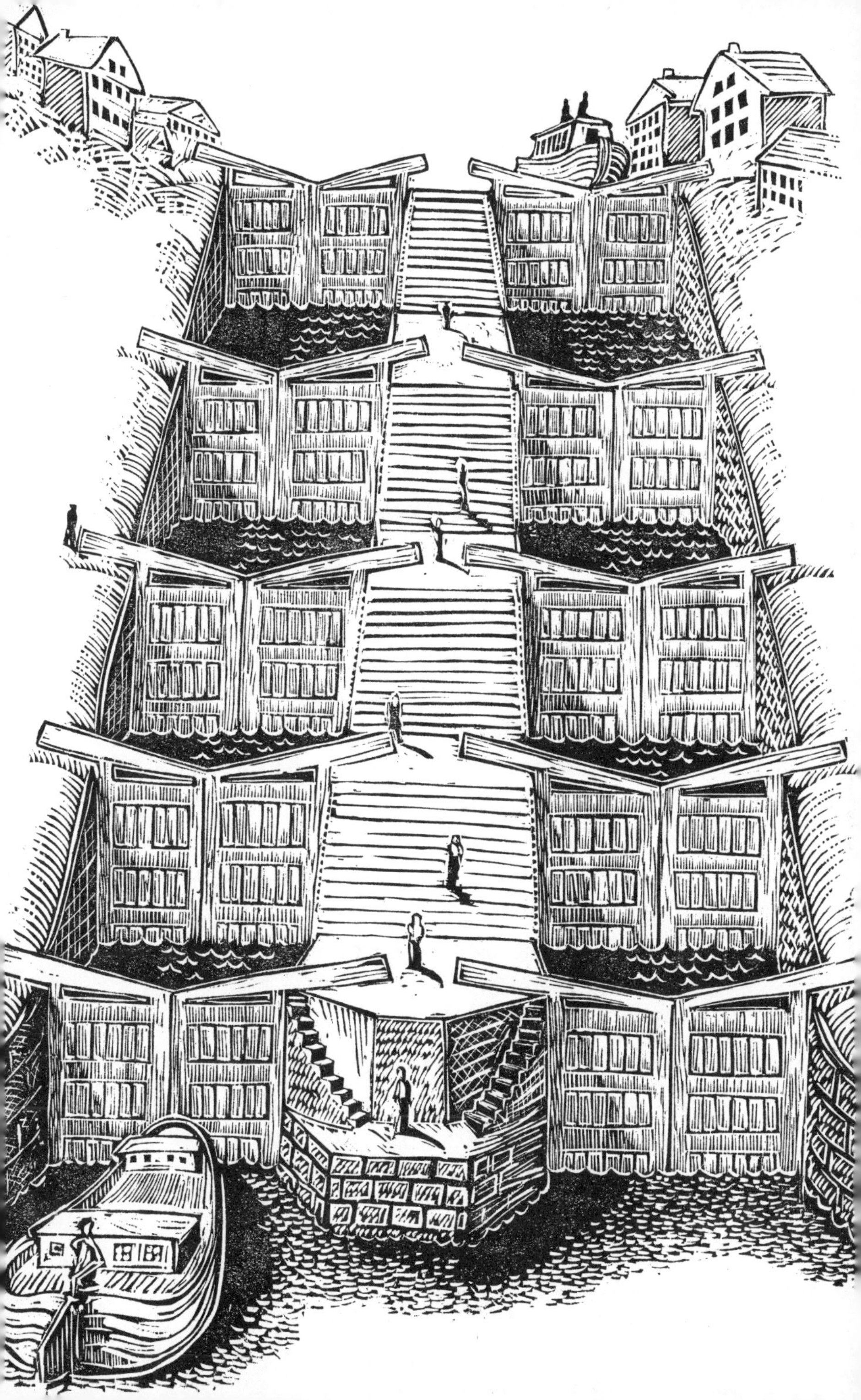

inches. This is the only place on the Erie that a twin flight of locks will be used. But without it, boats could become so jammed up while waiting to pass through the locks, it would take days to unsnarl the bottleneck.

Before construction begins, twelve hundred laborers—mostly Irishmen—are hired for "twelve dollars a month and found." Initial attempts to cut out the rock with hand chisels prove both slow and discouraging. There's talk of trying out the newly invented Du Pont blasting powder. Nathan Roberts observes a satisfying demonstration with this ammunition and promptly orders five hundred dollars worth. From now on, Du Pont's product will be used exclusively.

Roberts insists that the "powder monkeys," those who work with the explosives, take great care in preparing for a blast. First a hole is drilled in the rock by hand. Then it is filled with the coarse black powder and tamped down with clay. A twist of brown paper soaked in saltpeter is inserted for the fuse. At the warning cry "Look out!" the paper is ignited, and the workers dart quickly out of range of the hurtling stones.

In spite of all precautions, there are many accidents. The workers get careless, taking reckless chances. Sometimes a fuse fizzles out. When the blaster rushes back to relight it, he's blown up with the rock. Others are felled by flying fragments. There are days when the number of killed and wounded resembles the casualty list after a fierce battle.

Inhabitants of Lockport soon become accustomed to the continual noise of the blasting. They, too, find it's necessary to seek shelter quickly when an explosion occurs. One local resident remarks that "it sounds like Independence Day, Muster Day, and the thunders of Doomsday, all in one."

Another challenge confronting the contractors in this area is how to remove the rubble that accumulates from the gigantic explosions. At first the laborers fill wheelbarrows with the debris and shove them uphill to the level land above. But the broken rock piles up faster than the men can get rid of it. One inventive worker, Orange H. Dibble, devises a horse-operated derrick. By placing the derrick high above the cut where the blast occurs, a wooden bucket can be lowered and filled with the rubble. Then it's quickly raised and dumped on the bank. Because they save both time and labor, derricks are set up every seventy feet along the ridge overlooking the canal cut.

While work continues—and at a pace faster than anyone had hoped for—the laborers add another verse to their song about the Big Ditch:

"*We are cutting the Ditch through the rocks,*
Through the rocks across the state by heck!
We are cutting the Ditch through the rocks,

And we'll finish her off with stone locks,
From the rocks across the state, by heck!
From the rocks across the state."

Meanwhile, De Witt Clinton now devotes all his time to the waterway project. As chairman of the commission, he spends weeks during this summer and fall of 1823 riding along the canal route to inspect the work being done. He confers with the engineers about construction problems, settles minor disputes, and is never too hurried to encourage individual laborers. The erect figure on the gray horse becomes a familiar sight to all who are involved with the canal. And on October 8 the proud chairman presides over festivities in Albany to celebrate the opening of the eastern section. The canal at last is linked to the Hudson River.

Within state legislative circles, however, Clinton's political enemies have maneuvered many lawmakers into believing that De Witt Clinton is seeking glory only for himself. The powerful Albany Regency wants to give their own friends places of importance in canal jobs; "political patronage," it's called. They hope to make Clinton's great achievement a means for his downfall. By April 1824 a devious plot has been devised to discredit the man who has become a hero to so many people in New York State. Victory Birdseye, representative from Onondaga County, introduces a resolution to remove De Witt Clinton as chairman of the canal commission.

Stunned, Senator Henry Cunningham of Montgomery County jumps to his feet, eyes flashing with anger. "When the contemptible party strifes of the present day shall have passed by," he shouts, "the pen of the future historian, in better days and better times, will do him justice, and erect to his memory a proud monument of fame, as imperishable as the splendid works which owe their origin to his genius and perseverance."

The senator's impassioned words have little effect. The resolution is passed. The Albany Regency has done its work well; only three senators vote against it. On the final day of the session the assembly adopts the measure by an overwhelming majority. De Witt Clinton is now stripped of all authority over the canal.

Opponents of the former governor and "Clinton's Big Ditch" have not reckoned with the outburst of public indignation that follows this move. Thurlow Weed, editor of the Rochester *Telegraph*, denounces the resolution as "a deed which will ever blacken the annals of the State. . . . Every contemptible effort to rob Mr. Clinton of his well-earned fame serves only to identify him still more indissolubly with these great national works."

Mass rallies and protest meetings are held throughout the state to criticize the legislators who participated in such a despicable act. On April 19 an angry crowd of more than ten thousand people gathers in Albany's City Hall Park. They listen attentively to a long address by Charles G. Haines in which he details the progress of the canal. "Already we begin to feel its vast influence," he says, "as it strengthens the union of the East and the West, giving new life and vigor to agriculture and manufactures. . . . No wonder all Europe is astonished at the boldness of the state which undertakes, and is rapidly finishing, such works."

Then Mr. Haines asks, "Who devoted toilsome days and sleepless nights to demonstrate, by every argument, the practicability and advantages of the Great Western Canal? . . . Who, after he became the chief magistrate of this state, identified his administration with this work, and risked its duration on the success of the project? *De Witt Clinton is the man!*"

In conclusion, the speaker introduces eight resolutions that condemn the legislature's act as "degrading to the state, a violation of justice, and an outrage on public opinion." Noisy acclaim follows the reading of these resolutions, and they are delivered personally to Mr. Clinton.

After receiving them, the former governor remarks: "I know of no event that has a more powerful demand on my gratitude than the proceedings of the citizens of New York. . . . The approbation of a meeting so numerous and respectable is a reward that ought to satisfy the most aspiring ambition."

As public sentiment gathers momentum throughout this summer of 1824, there's much talk about returning De Witt Clinton to the office of governor. At the party convention in September he is nominated; in the November election he wins by a landslide. His opponents now agree with Martin Van Buren's estimate of the situation that "there is such a thing in politics as killing a man too dead."

The new governor's first act is to announce that despite all delays, the Erie Canal will definitely be completed by the fall of 1825—less than one year from now.

CHAPTER 9

Anticipating a Celebration

1825

With the coming of this new year—1825—Governor Clinton learns that the tolls collected during the past twelve months have amounted to more than three hundred thousand dollars. He is astounded. The amount is far in excess of his greatest hopes—and the canal is still to be completed. For the governor the past seven years have been ones of struggle and heartache. So many obstacles to overcome! Enemies of the project had been certain that it would be a financial failure. Now it appears that the monetary success of the waterway is assured.

However, no accurate method has yet been devised for determining the tolls. So far, collectors have only made casual estimates. The commissioners have agreed that the cost for boats using the canal is to be decided by the weight of the cargo and the number of miles traveled. Governor Clinton now consults with several supervisors; together they rig up a device called a weighlock, the first of its kind in America.

Though crude in appearance, the weighlock proves to be amazingly accurate. It is a ribbed cradle, designed to be set within a lock. The boat floats into the cradle, and the water is drained out, enabling the toll collector to measure the precise weight of both the craft and its cargo. Once this is recorded, and the toll paid, the weighlock is again filled with water, and the boat emerges on the canal to continue its passage.

Three weighlocks are installed—one at Troy, another at Utica, and a third at Syracuse. All boats entering the canal will have to pass through one of these ports; thus no captain can escape paying toll. The weighlocks are operated around the clock; only

four minutes are required for an individual craft to complete the procedure. Yet long lines soon begin to build up. At times there are as many as sixty or seventy boats waiting to be weighed.

Early in June the final construction work at Lockport is momentarily interrupted by the arrival of a distinguished visitor. The French hero of the American Revolutionary War, the Marquis de Lafayette, is touring the nation at the invitation of President James Monroe, an invitation issued before Monroe left office earlier this year. After viewing awesome Niagara Falls, he expresses a desire to see the waterway that the state of New York is building.

Governor Clinton provides a special boat, and the Frenchman enters the canal at Lockport. As a welcoming gesture, the construction gangs plant gunpowder every few feet along the sheer rock wall near the town. When the fuses are ignited, splinters of rock fly through the air. The noisy explosions at second intervals greet Lafayette as he enters the town. After the barrage is over, the guest smiles broadly and remarks, "The very rocks rend to welcome me."

Later in the day Lafayette refers to his visit at Niagara Falls and the twin flight of locks he has just inspected. "Lockport and the County of Niagara," he declares, "contain the greatest natural and artificial wonders, second only to the wonders of freedom and equal rights."

The visitor's secretary is likewise amazed at what he has witnessed and confides to his diary:

I have nowhere seen the activity and industry of man brought into operation against natural difficulties as in this young village. . . . In the midst of these encroachments of civilization on savage nature, that great canal is proceeding with a rapidity which seems to mark the hand of union, and will at the same time diffuse life and abundance in the deserts through which it passes.

Once the festivities are over at Lockport, construction continues on schedule. As the laborers move closer to Buffalo, the contractors plot a new way to speed up the work. A barrel of whiskey is placed at some distance ahead of the crew, but near enough so they can see it. When the men reach the barrel, they are allowed to take time out for drinks all around. Then it's back to work until they reach the next barrel. The shovels now fly faster than ever. There is little doubt that they'll finish on time, perhaps even a few days ahead of schedule.

Late in August the commissioners confirm reports that the canal will be completed by October. The date for the formal opening is set for October 26. This announcement throws people living along the canal line into a frenzy of wild excitement. They can talk of little else. For those who have dreamed of migrating west, it's the greatest news in many years.

Politicians in New York City who have long opposed the waterway now reverse themselves. With the canal an accomplished fact, they realize how wrong their opposition to its construction was. As a kind of belated apology, they plan the biggest celebration the city has ever known.

On September 7 William Bayard and John Pintard hold a meeting to organize a committee of the Corporation of the City of New York. Its members will plan and supervise the elaborate ceremonies to commemorate the completion of the pathway west and to honor the man who has spearheaded the project. It is decided that the theme of the celebration will be "the wedding of the waters." Water from Lake Erie is to be transported along the canal and mixed with that of the Atlantic Ocean.

Because the parade of boats will start in Buffalo, Aldermen King and Davis are sent out to that village to make certain that everything there is in readiness for what promises to be a memorable day. In addition, letters are dispatched to all the communities along the waterway, urging officials to plan appropriate ceremonies.

The New York committee is unaware that trade guilds and citizens' groups in the various settlements are already hard at work, vying to outdo one another in festive decorations. Ever since early summer, when it was first rumored that the canal would be finished this year, celebrations have been planned.

Artillery is being lined up. Bunting and flags are collected to set along the canal. In nearby forests there's a noisy clatter of tools as men construct hundreds of transparencies to illuminate the waters. The transparencies are oblong wooden boxes in the sides of which messages of congratulations are carved. Inside each box a lighted whale-oil lantern will be placed, so that at night the phrases can easily be read as the procession of boats glides along. Some of the longer transparencies will form archways over the water.

In the midst of all this activity, newsmen continue to write articles in praise of New York State's great achievement. The canal commissioners' financial report is widely quoted. Tolls collected during the summer months have now totaled over half a million dollars. It's an amount that amazes even the most skeptical. Three thousand boats, eight thousand men, and nine thousand horses are currently employed in transporting passengers and freight on the waterway. Officials at Albany announce that wholesale business has quadrupled since the eastern section was opened two years ago.

On October 8 the editor of the Buffalo *Emporium and General Advertiser* anticipates the great celebration by writing:

It will be a proud day in the history of New York, such as has not occurred since the Declaration of our country's Independence. Well may New York rejoice in an achievement that would add glory to the most powerful nation on earth.

Eight days before the procession of boats is scheduled to leave Buffalo, the Rochester *Telegraph* gives an enthusiastic proclamation to its readers:

The work is finished! Our brightest, highest hopes are all consummated. Let the shouts of triumph be heard from Erie to the Atlantic, and from the Atlantic resound back to Erie. Let the air be made vocal with our paeans of exultation and gratitude.

By the third week in October arrangements are complete for the firing of a "grand salute" to inform the people of New York City that the first boat to journey the entire length of the canal has entered the waterway. From Buffalo to Albany and down the banks of the Hudson River to the Atlantic, a string of cannon has been placed, twelve miles apart, along the canal. Upon hearing the opening blast from the cannon at Buffalo, the next gunner to the east will sound off—and so on down the line until the news is received in New York City. A message will be returned to Buffalo in the same way. To insure that the cannon are properly handled, veteran artillerymen will fire them. Many of the 32-pounders are those used by Commodore Perry's fleet in the victorious Battle of Lake Erie during the War of 1812.

On the evening of October 25 an entourage of private coaches pulls into the village of Buffalo. Accompanied by a number of dignitaries, Governor Clinton has arrived to make the inaugural journey down the Erie Canal and on to New York City for "the wedding of the waters." Now everything is in readiness for the greatest jubilation ever witnessed in this young nation.

CHAPTER 10

The Wedding of the Waters

1825

Long before dawn tints the eastern sky on this crisp clear morning of October 26, 1825, great throngs of people begin assembling at Buffalo. Men, women, children of all ages stream in from miles around, anxious to be a part of today's historic events.

Out in the canal basin is moored the *Seneca Chief*, a packet specially built for the inaugural journey. On the deckside facing the towpath are two large oil paintings. One shows the scene that will soon take place—the harbor with the lead boat ready to depart on her epic-making trip. In the foreground of the second painting is the figure of Governor Clinton, dressed in a Roman toga, standing beside a lock gate that he has just flung open. Beside the painting is a keg with an eagle drawn in flight and the inscription "Water of Lake Erie." The keg has been filled from the lake and will be emptied into the Atlantic Ocean during "the wedding of the waters" ceremony.

To symbolize the opening of the West, the *Seneca Chief*'s cargo includes potash from Detroit and Buffalo, whitefish from Lake Erie, flour and butter from Michigan and Ohio, and a canoe fashioned by Indians on the shore of Lake Superior. In addition, there is native red cedar and bird's-eye maple ordered by the Corporation of the City of New York. The wood will be used for making boxes to hold the medals struck in commemoration of the celebration.

About nine o'clock the public procession forms in front of the red-brick courthouse. Striking up a martial air, the town band leads off. The musicians are followed by the beaver-hatted dignitaries, Captain Rathburn's Company of Riflemen, and various groups of mechanics and tradesmen displaying large banners to identify their individual societies. Upon reaching the dock, Governor Clinton, Lieutenant Governor James Tallmadge, their staffs, and several village committee members go aboard amid cheers from the spectators.

Standing on the speakers' platform facing the boat is Jesse Hawley, famed for the newspaper articles he wrote more than eighteen years ago suggesting a canal to link Lake Erie with the Hudson. When the crowd quiets, Hawley begins his address. He speaks of the canal as a matter of state pride, "A work that will constitute the lever of industry, population and wealth to our Republic—a pattern for our Sister States to imitate."

Promptly at ten o'clock the first 32-pounder is discharged, signaling that the boats are underway. Now the message is passed from cannon to cannon down the line. Heading the procession is the *Seneca Chief*, pulled through the water by a team of four gray horses, driven along the towpath. Following behind are the *Superior*, the *Commodore Perry* (a freight boat), the *Buffalo*, and *Noah's Ark*. This last craft has been fitted out to portray the wilderness as it was before the white man came. Aboard are two young Seneca Indian lads, with two eagles, a bear, two deer, a beaver, a cage of wild birds, and a tank of fish.

As the flotilla moves out from the dock and into the canal, a great roar arises from the crowd of people lining the banks. The band blares. Captain Rathburn's riflemen add to the noisy confusion with a salvo of volleys. The first official voyage on the newly completed waterway has begun.

Over at Lockport, festivities started at sunrise this morning with a thirteen-gun salute. By nine o'clock a procession of the town's leading citizens walks out toward the locks where masses of people have gathered to watch the history-making ascent. Waiting at the eastern edge of the locks is the *William C. Bouck*, filled with a group of celebrities, including all the canal commissioners.

Shortly after ten, the report of the signal cannon is heard, announcing that the canal has been opened at Buffalo. The *Bouck* begins to move upward through the first lock while bands play, artillery gunners fire round after round, and powder blasts are deliberately set to echo through the rocky canyon. The crowd marvels as the boat ascends the steep flight of five locks.

Once the craft reaches the top of this mighty chasm, John Birdsall, aboard the *Bouck*, steps to the deck railing and shouts to the cheering hundreds, "The last barrier is passed. We now have risen to the level of Lake Erie and have before us navigation open to its waters!" The vessel then proceeds west to Pendleton where it awaits the arrival of the flotilla traveling east.

It is not long before the *Seneca Chief* comes into view. After ceremonial greetings are exchanged, the *Bouck* joins the line of boats heading for Lockport. Here they dock along the towpath above the locks. As Governor Clinton steps off the *Seneca*, a shout arises from the jubilant crowd. Here's the man who has made this waterway a reality.

The celebrities are entertained with a sumptuous banquet at Lockport's Washington House; the feast and toasts that follow continue through most of the afternoon. After dusk the guests return to the waiting boats and experience their first ride down the five flights of locks before continuing eastward.

Meanwhile everyone in New York City has heard that the canal is officially open. The message relayed by cannon fire arrived exactly eighty-one minutes after the 32-pounder was fired at Buffalo. The return salute was received in approximately the same length of time. Officials are pleased that the plan they devised has worked so well.

When the procession of boats nears Rochester on Thursday afternoon, they are met by the *Young Lion of the West*. On board this craft are a pair of eagles, a fox, two wolves, a fawn, and four raccoons.

A sentinel on the deck of the *Young Lion* calls out: "Who comes there?"

"Your brothers from the west, on the waters of the Great Lakes," answers the sentinel on the *Seneca Chief*.

"By what means have they been diverted so far from their natural course?"

"By the channel of the Grand Erie Canal."

"By whose authority, and by whom, was the work of such magnitude accomplished?"

"By the authority and by the enterprise of the patriotic people of the state of New York."

Now that the dialogue is concluded, the *Young*

Lion from the West joins the line of craft moving into the Rochester basin. Here the dignitaries are greeted and conducted to the Presbyterian church for prayers and congratulations. A dinner at Christopher's Mansion House follows before the guests depart at seven thirty.

The flotilla is following a carefully arranged schedule with a stopover at nearly every port along the line. The celebrations are much the same. Archways garlanded with flowers and evergreens span the canal; flags and bunting add a patriotic touch. When the boats dock, cannon thunder a salute to the inaugural delegation. Spectators flock to the towpath and crowd on the bridges, jostling each other in their eagerness to hear the speeches of welcome and response. Usually there's a festive meal with toasts to the honored guest. And as the long procession moves eastward after dark, hundreds of transparencies illuminate the water with their messages of appreciation for De Witt Clinton.

During the next few days there are stops at Palmyra, Lyons, Clyde, Port Byron, Weedsport, Syracuse, Manlius, Rome, Utica, Little Falls, and Schenectady. Each offers its hospitality—some with more originality than others. Between most settlements, there is still a vast wilderness. In many places deep forests edge the towpath; the passengers are fascinated by the wild animals, the profusion of flowers and shrubs to be seen as the boats glide by.

On Wednesday morning, November 2, one week after leaving Buffalo, the *Seneca Chief* leads the flotilla into the Albany basin for a day-long celebration, the most elaborate one yet. The highlight for Governor Clinton comes when a handsome oil portrait of himself is unveiled in the Assembly Chamber, the very room where he has endured so many insults from his political opponents. All the unhappy times are now forgotten in this hour of joyous tribute.

It is nearly ten o'clock Thursday morning before everything is in readiness for the ride down the Hudson River. Immense crowds line the riverfront to cheer the procession now forming. Eight steamboats will tow the flotilla down to New York City. At a given signal the fleet gets underway, accompanied by dozens of small craft whose owners are anxious to become a part of the historic journey.

Today there are to be no stops, but thousands are standing on the shoreline, waving flags and shouting with excitement as the vessels pass. Noisy artillery salutes are fired at Hudson, Catskill, and Hyde Park. When the flotilla approaches Poughkeepsie, huge signal fires are lighted, casting a bright red glare over the hills and water. West Point, situated high above the river, celebrates with a twenty-four-gun volley as the first boats come in sight. It's late though, and the passengers retire soon after passing the United States Military Academy.

At seven o'clock on this climactic Friday, November 4, 1825, the squadron moves into New York harbor as the sun rises in the east, shining down on the largest collection of boats ever assembled here. Steaming up the East River to the Brooklyn Navy Yard, the fleet is given a thunderous salute. Then the parade turns and heads back to the Battery for the "Grand Aquatic Display." Forty-six vessels, lavishly decorated with flowers, bunting, and flags surround the canalboats and perform a series of intricate maneuvers.

After receiving another salute from the Battery, the squadron of vessels steams out toward the ocean for a ceremonial rendezvous with the United States schooner *Porpoise*, anchored at Sandy Hook since last night. As the boats approach Sandy Hook, they are met by the steamship *Washington.* From the deck of that vessel booms a voice, asking, "Whence come you, and where are you bound?"

The sentinel aboard the *Seneca Chief* gives the answer, "From Lake Erie—and bound for Sandy Hook!"

Governor Clinton and the special committees now transfer to the *Washington* for the long-awaited Wedding of the Waters, while the other boats form a circle around the two vessels. Guns roar and spectators cheer as the governor hoists the keg of Lake Eric water to his shoulder. In this moment of greatest triumph, he slowly and solemnly pours the contents into the Atlantic Ocean.

When the last drop is gone, Clinton turns to the assembled dignitaries. "The solemnity, at this place on the first arrival of vessels from Lake Erie," he says, "is intended to indicate and commemorate the navigable communication, which has been accomplished between our Mediterranean seas and the Atlantic Ocean, in about eight years, to the extent of more than four hundred and twenty-five miles, by the wisdom, public spirit, and energy of the people of the state of New York; and may the God of the Heavens and the Earth smile most propitiously on this work, and render it subservient to the best interests of the human race."

Dr. Samuel Latham Mitchill, noted for his collection of the rare and the curious, now steps to the side of the boat carrying a box filled with bottles of river water. One after another, he empties them into the Atlantic—water from the Ganges and Indus of Asia; the Nile and the Gambia of Africa; the Thames, the Seine, the Rhine, and the Danube of Europe; the Mississippi and the Columbia of North America; the Orinoco, the La Plata, and the Amazon of South America. In the address that follows, he proclaims that all the great waters of the world are now united.

With the "wedding" concluded, the ships return

WATER
LAKE ERIE

to dock at Pier One on the East River. Amidst all the excitement a reporter aboard the *Washington* dashes off an account for his newspaper:

Never before was there such a fleet collected and so superbly decorated; and it is very possible that a display so grand, so beautiful, and we may even add, so sublime, will never be witnessed again. We know of nothing with which it can be compared. . . .

Back at the Battery "the Grand Procession" is lining up, a parade of some five thousand participants, the longest ever assembled in America. When Governor Clinton and the special guests take their seats on the reviewing stand, a thunderous artillery blast signals the start of the marchers.

There are bands, clubs, and trade guilds, military units and civilian groups. Two hundred floats represent the bakers, butchers, cobblers, tanners, cordwainers, hatters, and candlestick makers. Most attention-getting is the Typographical Society float—a wagon on which are mounted two hand-powered presses, where operators are busy turning out copies of an ode written in honor of the occasion. These are tossed out to the fifty thousand cheering spectators and eagerly snatched up as mementoes of the historic day.

After the parade ends, there are parties all over

town to honor Governor Clinton. Many families have brought baskets of food, and the fields around Broadway become one mammoth picnic ground. Others crowd into public restaurants where special dishes are featured—the favorite being "Canal Beef," transported from the west by way of the Erie Canal. When darkness falls, the city becomes a fairyland of light. Candles and torches illuminate hundreds of public buildings, stores, and homes. As the crowds mill through the streets, the name "Clinton" is on everyone's lips.

The celebration is climaxed by a dazzling display of fireworks on the City Hall lawn. Thousands of fireballs cross and crisscross each other against the night sky, only to rain down in a shower of stars. Most spectacular of all are the gigantic rockets fired at an angle, so that their red, white, and blue lights drift into the Hudson River.

Late tonight Governor Clinton returns to the *Seneca Chief*. In his hand is a copy of the memoir written by Cadwallader Colden at the request of the mayor of the city of New York. After this long day of excitement and triumph, the governor finds sleep impossible. Instead he pores over the lengthy account of the inaugural journey, reliving each hour of the ten-day celebration. When he reaches the final page, tears stream down his cheeks. Mr. Colden has concluded with these words:

The authors and builders—the heads who planned, and the hands who executed this stupendous work, deserve a perennial monument; and they will have it. To borrow an expression from the highest of all sources, "the works which they have done, these will bear witness of them." Europe begins already to admire—American can never forget to acknowledge, that THEY HAVE BUILT THE LONGEST CANAL IN THE WORLD IN THE LEAST TIME, WITH THE LEAST EXPERIENCE, FOR THE LEAST MONEY, AND TO THE GREATEST PUBLIC BENEFIT.

CHAPTER II

Canal Travel

1825–1850

Nothing in this young nation has caused such a sensation as the opening of the Erie Canal. Europeans, too, are very much impressed, particularly the British. The English publication, *Blackwood's Magazine*, whose editor has never been partial to this country, surprises everyone here by writing:

There does not exist at this time, on the whole face of the earth, any district more flourishing, more improving, more enterprizing, than the State of New York. The great canal, which beggars to insignificance all similar undertakings in the old world, and in point of extent is the largest line of continued labour in the world, after the wall of China, is of itself a sufficient proof and illustration of the fact.

Now upstate New Yorkers are seized by excitement—"canawl fever," it's called. Some say the Irish work gangs began pronouncing it "canawl." Others believe it was descendants of the Dutch who twisted the sound. Whatever the origin, "canawl" it remains.

Weather permitting, the navigable season lasts from late February until early December. By 1835 it's estimated that four thousand vessels are plying these waters. People from all over the country are finding this mode of transportation far more pleasurable than the jouncing stagecoach. There's a constant stream of emigrants heading west to find new homes. Even European travelers are booking passage on the packets to see the country about which they have read.

Commerce is stimulated far beyond anyone's hopes. Cargo boats going out to Buffalo are filled with guns, needles, knives, bolts of cloth, whalebone corsets, and hundreds of other articles made in New England and needed by the pioneers. Craft traveling east carry fresh farm produce and timber to the coastal cities. The tolls collected have exceeded all expectations.

There's no longer the danger that lack of communication will split the country. Back in 1815, De Witt Clinton asserted that "this canal, as to the extent of its route, as to the countries which it connects, and as to the consequences which it will produce is without a parallel in the history of mankind." Now that prophecy has become a reality.

Queen of the waterway is the packet, a passenger boat that takes precedence over all other vessels when entering locks or passing midstream. This aristocrat is easy to recognize as it comes gliding along the canal. Though narrow in width, it's usually seventy or eighty feet long. The boxlike cabin is mounted on a deck and surrounded by a high railing with only a twelve-inch passageway between the two. A row of tiny windows, all gaily curtained, gives travelers a good view of the passing scenery. Most packets are painted in dazzling colors. Inscribed on the bow is the name of the vessel; among the more prominent are *Fair Play*, *Pirate's Pride*, *Rip Van Winkle*, *Merry Fiddler*, *Try to Catch Me*, *Stormy Lass*, and *Sea Rover*.

When a packet is about to leave its dock, the captain calls out "Cleat up," and a deckhand fastens the tow line to a cleat in the middle of the bow. One hundred feet ahead on the towpath, the driver signals that his trio of horses or mules is ready. The line goes taut as the boat begins to move, guided by the steersman who stands at the tiller bar and manipulates the rudder. At relay stations situated beside the canal, the team is changed every ten miles, enabling the packet to travel eighty or ninety miles a day—far faster than anything else on the waterway.

The interior of the cabin, often called "the saloon," is a single low-ceilinged room set with two rows of tables for dining. A small cubbyhole at the rear serves as the cook's galley as well as his living quarters. Here he prepares lavish meals for the passengers, meals that include several kinds of meat and fish, potatoes, a varied assortment of vegetables, and a choice of cakes and pies.

During daylight hours travelers often mount the narrow stairway leading to the upper deck. Sitting on low-backed benches or chairs, they watch the passing panorama of forests and fields mingled with the colorful excitement of canal-side villages.

At night the saloon becomes the sleeping area. Mattresses are spread out on the tables, and narrow bunks are installed along the walls, three tiers high. In the more luxurious packets, a heavy velvet curtain is stretched across the center of the room to separate the men's quarters from the women's.

After taking a trip on one of the packets, the British writer, Charles Dickens, describes his reaction to the sudden transformation in the saloon:

Going below, I found suspended on either side of the cabin, three long tiers of hanging bookshelves, designed apparently for volumes of the small octavo size. Looking with great attention at these contrivances (wondering to find such literary preparations in such a place), I descried on each shelf a sort of microscopic sheet and blanket; then I began to dimly comprehend that the passengers were the library, and that they were to be arranged edgewise on these shelves till morning.

Nevertheless, Dickens adds, "There was much in this mode of traveling which I heartily enjoyed at the time and look back upon with much pleasure . . . the exquisite beauty of the opening day, when light came glancing off from everything; the gliding on at night so noiselessly . . . the shining out of the bright stars undisturbed by any noise of wheels. . . . All these were pure delights."

To the packet captain, speed is very important. Though the legal limit is four miles an hour, he sometimes steps up to six or seven. Knowing he is liable to a ten-dollar penalty, he jumps ashore, tosses the money at the toll collector, and continues on his way. The captain will earn more by making good time than he's lost by paying the fine.

The line boat is used exclusively by the pioneer and his family going west, since the packets allow only passengers with hand luggage. On this vessel the emigrants bring all their possessions on board; they are even allowed to set up cookstoves on the deck. Here meals are prepared amid stacked furniture, pet dogs, crates of chickens, and bundles of clothing. No sleeping facilities are provided. Those on the line boat simply curl up wherever they can. Travel is slow, since the tow horses are usually old nags and are never replaced by a fresh team during the trip. Thirty to forty miles a day is considered speedy. Even so, the smooth ride of a line boat is preferable to bumping along in a wagon.

Most numerous on the canal are the freighters that haul cargo from one place to another. Known as "bullheads," these boats are characterized by their rounded bow. Though they carry no passengers, there's often a stable aboard. While two mules (called "hayburners") are pulling the freighter through the water, their replacements are resting or munching feed. Many owners and animals live out their years on these boats, having no other home. Occasionally two or more empty cargo boats will hook up with a full freighter so that one team of mules pulls all three craft. Canal watchers call this procession a "hoodle-dasher."

The clumsiest contraption using the waterway is the timber raft, a craft particularly disliked by boat captains. The raft consists of anywhere from five to ten sections of logs lashed together and towed through the water by a team of mules. Aboard is a crew of four men who steer the logs with long poles. Passing one of these timber rafts is a tiresome procedure and often slows up the flow of traffic. Canal regulations stipulate that upon reaching a lock, the sections must be unhitched and passed through separately, alternating with any vessels that come along. Everyone agrees that these long delays are exasperating.

Then there's the shantyboat, a familiar sight along the canal. It's usually anchored in some basin and remains there the year around, unless its occupants have a desire to move elsewhere. They seldom do. The shanty resembles a crude houseboat with its one-room hovel attached to the deck surface. Sometimes there's even a lean-to porch in the rear. Children of families living on shantyboats love the gypsylike existence—fishing when they want to, roaming over nearby fields to hunt for wild berries, or taking a dip in the water whenever the whim strikes.

The horse or mule team that walks the towpath pulling the boat through the water is the responsibility of the driver, better known as the "hoggee." Most of the drivers are boys—some as young as fourteen. Each hoggee walks two six-hour shifts or "tricks" daily, no matter what the weather. In his spare time he must feed and water his team, repair harness, and treat any sores that have developed on the animals. In addition, he cooks his own meals and sleeps wherever he can find space—usually behind a packing box.

Despite his youth, the hoggee's work is very exacting. With boats often passing each other on the canal, it's easy for towlines to become tangled; the lad must make sure this doesn't happen. Occasionally one of the horses will panic, shy away, and land in the canal.

Then the hoggee detaches the towline, swims the frightened animal to the nearest horse ramp, and returns him to the team. All this, while the boat captain is shouting a barrage of insults.

The boy's salary is ten dollars a month, the wages being paid when the canal closes late in the fall. Some never receive a penny. A captain will often deliberately mistreat the lad toward the close of the season, so he'll run away without collecting his money. By 1848 it's reported that ten thousand boys are employed as hoggees on the Erie.

Among the men who keep the boats moving, fighting has become very popular. Loading and unloading heavy cargo is hard work. Wages are low. And the slow pace of travel is a constant irritant. When the vessel docks after a long trip, the crew is frequently in a belligerent mood. There are often many bloodied noses before nightfall. Boat captains pride themselves on hiring "bullies"—men who are experts with their fists. Thus their boats will be well represented when a brawl breaks out.

In the operation of the waterway, one of the busiest persons is the "lock-keep." On duty seven days a week, he opens and shuts the huge wooden gates that allow traffic to pass from one level to another. He uses his shanty as a combined office and home, snatching what catnaps he can between bugle calls from waiting boats. The more enterprising lock-keep has

a supply of groceries to sell, a bar to cheer "canawllers" on frosty nights, and he even peddles remedies for ailing men and mules. Sometimes a jam occurs among vessels waiting to lock through. Fights break out among the crewmen, and the lock-keep then acts as referee. He receives twenty-five dollars a month in pay and "lodgings free for family and self."

Maintenance of the canal requires constant vigilance. Eel, moles, and mink are forever digging small holes. But the burrowing muskrat is the most troublesome animal. Rewards are frequently offered for catching a muskrat, dead or alive.

Watchmen, known as "towpath walkers," patrol a ten-mile section every day, inspecting the aqueducts and locks for any signs of damage, looking for erosion in the banks and leaks in the channel. Every towpath walker carries "whisks" of twisted straw. If he spots even the smallest whirl in the waters, he wades in to plug the hole with straw, firmly tamping it down.

Whenever a serious break occurs, a call goes out for the "hurry-up boat," an emergency craft that takes priority over all other vessels on the canal, even the packet. Horses pulling the hurry-up boat are allowed to gallop at top speed along the towpath. People come running from all directions to watch the boat rushing toward the break.

In addition to its importance as a mode of transportation for both passengers and freight, the Erie

Canal has opened up a whole new world for those living in the isolated communities of upstate New York. Before the coming of the waterway, the backwoodsman was practically in exile. Now there are floating grocery stores, tinkers' shops, penny museums, even bookstores and libraries that drift from one village to another. Most exciting of all are the showboats bringing theatrical companies to perform in local halls.

The official name of the waterway is the Erie Canal, though it's been called many others: the Big Ditch, the Great Western Canal, Clinton's Ditch, the Governor's Gully, Clinton's Folly, the Grand Erie Canal. Regardless of title, all America is impressed with what the canal has accomplished.

New York has emerged as the Empire State, realizing a prosperity never believed possible. Thousands of settlers are streaming west to build for the future. Trade between the states has united the country as nothing else could. All this—because of one man's courage, vision, and determination. De Witt Clinton's bold venture will be long remembered.

CHAPTER 12

Epilogue

From Then Till Now

"Canawl fever" lasted only about thirty years—from 1820 to 1850. But during this time the success of the New York waterway brought a rash of canal building in Illinois, Ohio, Indiana, Massachusetts, and Virginia. By the early 1850s there were forty-five hundred miles of navigable water in use in the United States. The Erie Canal, though, was the only one that proved to be a profit-making venture.

The coming of the railroads produced a drastic decline in canal traffic. When speed was essential, freight was shipped by rail rather than by water. Passenger travel fell off; the packets disappeared. Many canals were plagued by debt. There was no money for repairs, and the waterways were abandoned.

Not so the Erie. Here there was little competition from the railroads; it was still the easiest way through the barrier of the Appalachian Mountains to the west. By 1862 the Erie Canal had been enlarged several times. It was then seventy feet wide on the surface—almost twice the original width—and seven feet deep. During the Civil War the New York waterway provided the safest, most practical passage for moving the Union Army's men and supplies. As the years passed, freight shipments increased, and in 1882 all toll charges were abolished. The state had

made a total profit of more than fifty million dollars.

By the turn of the century it was more and more apparent that the canal was neither wide enough nor deep enough for heavy barges. In 1903 the legislature authorized a bond issue of 101 million dollars to build a network of waterways. Much of the old Erie was relocated, shifted from its former course, and combined with three shorter canals to form the New York State Barge Canal. Opened in 1918, its 525-mile length provides excellent transportation for modern freighters.

In 1926 a centennial celebration was held in Albany, New York, to commemorate the progress of the Erie—its development from a shallow waterway to a system capable of handling barges of up to three hundred tons. One of the commissioners that day noted that "the world has moved a long way since the first canal was opened, but the wonderful advancement seen in the engineering and construction field, the discoveries made in scientific research and our modern inventions, can in no way dim the glories of the 'Grand Canal' . . . nor can the canal's beneficent influence on the State and the Nation be overrated."

The color, the romance, the excitement of "canawling" have long since gone. Little remains of the original Erie Canal except a few crumbling locks, fragments of moss-covered aqueducts, and occasional stretches of channel, choked with cattails and filled with stagnant water. Yet these few relics recall a bold and heroic achievement, a legendary monument to Yankee inventiveness in an era when there was no power machinery, few tools, and "engineers" with only a meager knowledge of construction.

Today most historians agree that the Erie Canal had a profound impact on the development of the United States by opening up western lands, revolutionizing transportation, and making economic history.

Bibliography

Bobbé, Dorothie. *De Witt Clinton.* New York: Minton, Balch and Company, 1933.

Brunger, Eric. *The Grand Canal: New York's First Thruway.* Buffalo, New York: Buffalo and Erie County Historical Society, 1964.

Campbell, William W. *Life and Writings of DeWitt Clinton.* New York: Baker and Scribner, 1849.

Carmer, Carl. *The Hudson.* New York: Farrar and Rinehart, 1939.

Clinton, De Witt. *The Canal Policy of the State of New York.* Albany, New York: E. and E. Hosford, 1821.

———. *Remarks on the Proposed Canal, from Lake Erie to the Hudson River.* New York: Samuel Wood Sons, 1816.

Colden, Cadwallader D. *Memoir, Prepared at the Request of a Committtee of the Common Council of the City of New York.* New York: W. A. Davies, 1825.

Condon, George E. *Stars in the Water: The Story of the Erie Canal.* Garden City, New York: Doubleday and Company, 1974.

Dunbar, Seymour. *A History of Travel in America.* New York: Tudor Publishing Company, 1937.

Eaton, M. *Five Years on the Erie Canal.* Utica, New York: Bennett, Backus, and Hawley, 1845.

Geddes, George. *Origin and History of Measures That Led to Its* [The Erie Canal's] *Construction.* Buffalo Historical Society Publications, Volume 2, pages 263–304.

Goodrich, Carter. *Canals and American Economic Development.* New York: Columbia University Press, 1961.

Haines, Charles Glidden. *Considerations on the Great Western Canal from the Hudson to Lake Erie.* Brooklyn, New York: Spooner and Worthington, Printers, 1818.

———. *Public Documents Relating to the New York Canals.* New York: William A. Mercein, 1821.

Harlow, Alvin Fay. *Old Towpaths: The Story of the American Canal Era.* New York: D. Appleton and Company, 1926.

Hawley, Merwin S. *The Origin of the Erie Canal.* Buffalo Historical Society Publications. Volume 2, pages 227–261.

Hepburn, A. Barton. *Artificial Waterways and Commercial Development, with a History of the Erie Canal.* New York: The Macmillan Company, 1909.

Holbrook, Stewart H. *The Yankee Exodus.* New York: The Macmillan Company, 1950.

Hislop, Codman. *The Mohawk.* New York: Rinehart and Company, 1948.

Hosack, David. *Memoir of DeWitt Clinton, with an Appendix Containing Numerous Documents, Illustrative of the Principal Events of His Life.* New York: J. Seymour, 1829.

Johnson, Crisfield. *Centennial History of Erie County, New York.* Buffalo, New York: Matthews and Warren, 1876.

Kimball, Francis P. *New York—The Canal State: The Story*

of America's Great Water Route. Albany, New York: The Argus Press, 1937.

Laws of the State of New York in Relation to the Erie Canal, with Annual Reports of the Canal Commissions. Albany New York: J. Burl, 1825.

Matthews, Lois Kimball. *The Erie Canal and the Settlement of the West.* Buffalo Historical Society Publications. Volume 14, pages 189–203.

———. *The Holland Land Company and Canal Construction in Western New York.* Buffalo Historical Society Publications. Volume 14, pages 3–185.

McKlevey, Blake. *The Erie Canal: Mother of Cities.* New York History Society Quarterly. Volume 35, pages 55–71.

Miller, Nathan. *The Enterprise of a Free People: Aspects of Economic Development in New York State During the Canal Period,* 1792–1838. Ithaca, New York: Cornell University Press, 1962.

Payne, Robert. *The Canal Builders.* New York: The Macmillan Company, 1954.

Pearce, Mrs. John N. *The White House: An Historic Guide.* Washington, D.C.: The White House Historical Association, 1964.

Renwick, James. *Life of De Witt Clinton.* New York: Harper Brothers, 1859.

Riegel, Robert E. *America Moves West.* New York: Henry Holt and Company, 1956.

Shaw, Ronald E. *Erie Water West: A History of the Erie Canal, 1792–1854.* Lexington, Kentucky: University of Kentucky Press, 1966.

Smith, H. Perry. *History of the City of Buffalo and Erie County, with Biographical Sketches.* Syracuse, New York: D. Mason and Company, 1884.

Spafford, Horatio Gates. *A Pocket Guide for the Tourist and Traveler Along the Line of Canals.* New York: T. and J. Swords, 1824.

Stone, William Leete. *Narrative of the Festivities Observed in Honor of the Completion of the Grand Canal.* Prepared at the request of the Committee of the Corporation of the City of New York. New York: 1825.

Waggoner, Madeline Sadler. *The Long Haul West.* New York: G. P. Putnam's Sons, 1958.

Watson, Elkanah. *History of the Rise, Progress, and Existing Conditions of the Western Canals of New York from 1788 to 1819.* Albany, New York: D. Steele, 1820.

Whitford, Noble E. *History of the Canal System in the State of New York.* Two volumes. Albany, New York: Brandow Printing Company, 1906.

Wright, Benjamin Hall. *Origin of the Erie Canal: Services of Benjamin Wright.* Rome, New York: Sanford and Carr, 1870.

Wyld, Lionel D. *Low Bridge! Folklore and the Erie Canal.* Syracuse, New York: Syracuse University Press, 1962.

NEWSPAPERS

Albany *Gazette and General Advertiser*

Buffalo *Emporium*

Genesee Messenger

Rochester *Telegraph*

Index

ABOUT THE AUTHOR

Mary Kay Phelan's career as a writer began in response to questions from her two young sons. When she could not find a book that satisfied their demands for more information about the White House, she wrote one herself. And she has continued to write books that bring American history vividly to life. Among them are *Four Days in Philadelphia–1776; Midnight Alarm: The Story of Paul Revere's Ride;* and *Mr. Lincoln's Inaugural Journey*.

Born in Kansas, Mrs. Phelan was graduated from DePauw University in Indiana and received her master's degree in English from Northwestern University. She and her husband have produced historical films that are widely used in schools and libraries. The Phelans live in Davenport, Iowa, most of the year but enjoy their frequent travels in this country and in Europe.

ABOUT THE ARTIST

In the course of his research on WATERWAY WEST, David Frampton went to see the remains of the Erie Canal in Syracuse, New York. At the Erie Canal Museum, also in Syracuse, he saw many of the original tools that were used in the building of the canal.

Mr. Frampton was born in New York City. He was graduated from the Rhode Island School of Design, and received a master's degree in printmaking from the Pennsylvania State University. With his wife and two children he now lives in New Hampshire.